MW01286295

The Art of Hackamore Training

A **WESTERN HORSEMAN** BOOK

The Art of Hackamore Training

A Time-Honored Step in the Bridle-Horse Tradition

**Al Dunning and Benny Guitron
with Deanna Lally**

Photographs by Robert Dawson

Edited by Fran Devereux Smith

The Art of
Hackamore Training

Published by
WESTERN HORSEMAN magazine
2112 Montgomery St.
Fort Worth, TX 76107
817-737-6397

www.westernhorseman.com

Design, Typography, and Production
Globe Pequot Press
Guilford, Connecticut

Printing
Versa Press, Inc.
East Peoria, Illinois

©2012 MCC Magazines, LLC. All Rights Reserved.

This book is protected by federal copyright law. No material may be copied, faxed, electronically transmitted, reproduced or otherwise used without express, written permission. Requests must be submitted in writing to **Western Horseman**.

Manufactured in the United States of America

Third Printing: December 2013

ISBN 978-0-7627-8056-3

WESTERN HORSEMAN is a registered trademark of MCC Magazines, LLC.

Dedication and Acknowledgments

I'd like to dedicate this book to the great hackamore men of our past—Tony Amaral, Ray Hackworth, Don Dodge, Johnny Brazil, and many others. These horsemen, along with John Hoyt and Jim Paul, impacted my life and career, inspiring me to take up the reins and continue the hackamore tradition. It is my hope that *The Art of Hackamore Training* will honor all of them and other traditionalists who have kept the hackamore not only in their programs, but also in their hearts.

Al Dunning

To the horsemen and horses that have given me the opportunity…but mostly to my family.

Benny Guitron

Contents

Introduction

The sun sets over the lush grazing grounds of early 1800s California, bathing herds of cattle numbering greater than 400,000 head in the last of its warm light. A horseman astride a fine, responsive mount rides away. His wide-brimmed hat casts a distinctive shadow over his floral bandana and the shoulders of his bolero jacket. He wears fitted pants, unbuttoned from the knee down, showing his leather *botas,* or leggings, and large-roweled spurs, which display his status as a horseman who walks only should circumstance require. The bright sash he's donned boasts of his tradition and of loyalty to his Spanish roots.

The rider's hands work a horsehair *mecate* rein with skill and precision, communicating concise cues to his young *jaquima* (hackamore) horse. The horse feels the pull and release of the braided hackamore on his nose and jaw, and moves his body and feet willingly with swift athleticism—the vaquero's pride. Man and horse are a team.

This mount is not only a working partner who allows the vaquero to drive the herds and throw his reata, but also is an advertisement for the vaquero's skills as a horseman. As he draws a rein, the quick-footed horse gives his nose and spins or slides to a halt in a show even more eye-catching than the flashy Spanish clothing. To the native Indians the vaquero is a skilled tradesman—one to be revered.

The vaquero, however, is much more than a showy horseman; he is the product of secrets and traditions passed from fathers to sons for generations. He understands the patient progression of training a young horse and knows that the time required can no more be hurried than the change of seasons. The horseman takes equal pride in his equipment, in the fine, smooth braid of the hackamore, the fit of the *fiador* and feel of the mecate. These tools are not only the means of making his living, but also tools for displaying the very artistry born into him, as much so as the blood in his veins.

With his saddle horse turned loose in the corral for the night, the vaquero wipes down his tack and takes a round stick to the inside of the nose button of his hackamore, smoothing the sweat and dirt to a flat polish. Though tired from the long day, he kneels down to finish braiding the heel knot of the thin, quarter-inch *bosalito,* the light bosal he needs as he advances his hackamore horse through the evolution of a finished bridle horse, the same way his father did and his father's father before him.

Now those days and many of the vaquero ways are long gone, having given way to the steam engine, the Model T and the airplane. Today the luxury of unlimited tack to aid in training horses is available at the click of a button on high-speed Internet connections. Fast-paced generations have carried us far from our history and the time-honored customs of our founding horsemen-fathers. This loss of tradition and knowledge has left many ignorant of the old-time culture that colors the tightly braided hackamore still in use today.

In the following pages, we wish to share with you the art of training in la jaquima, the hackamore. Let us take you beneath these exercises and training drills to discover the true art of this mechanism, a process rich with heritage and patience. The hackamore, by design, cannot be manipulated by thoughtless hands to achieve any fine result. Only the skillful pull and release of a savvy trainer can coax a horse to give and move with the coveted softness.

Armed with such time-tested knowledge and one-foot-in-front-of-the-other diligence, you can develop a new skill set that opens doors of communication and trust with your horse, as well as builds a solid foundation for all the training to come. These old

practices are timeless, enabling fluid progression in horse training and heightened levels of performance.

With a better understanding of the hackamore's colorful history—how, why and by whom it was created, used and perfected—you can take the importance of this piece of equipment to heart in your own training program. The many different types and sizes of hackamores, coupled with the education of how and when to use each of them, can broaden your perspective and ability as a trainer, from that all-important first ride on a fresh colt through the entire journey of finishing your bridle horse.

These proven practices, once passed down from fathers to sons, have been dying out in recent generations. However, laid out in this book are those secrets—the methods and means of making a responsive, willing horse through proper gear, skilled hands, and sound training theory.

The lifestyle that birthed the venerated reined cow horse has faded into a dusty memory. But if you look closely, you can see that history woven into the patterns of the rawhide. Look closer still, and you find salt from the vaquero's sweat, the calluses of his hands, and the red of his blood in the details …in the very art of the hackamore.

Meet Benny

Born in Glendale, Calif., on February 12, 1948, Benny Guitron is the fifth of Felix Guitron Sr.'s six children. Young Guitron, inspired as a youth by the great horsemen of his day—Jimmy Williams, Harold Farren, Red Neal, Don Dodge and perhaps most significantly, vaquero trainer, Tony Amaral Sr.—became fired by a dream. Determined to achieve his dream, Guitron set out to be like those horsemen and to train horses in ways honorable to tradition. His eagerness to soak up whatever knowledge was available molded the aspiring young man into the all-around, renowned horsemen he is today.

Guitron Sr. played a crucial role in fanning the flames of his young son's aspirations. Having immigrated to California from Mexico, the elder Guitron worked hard to save money and eventually purchased his own spread in the Coachella Valley. Though Guitron Sr. farmed for a living, a passion for horses also was a part of his life.

Under their father's guidance, Benny Guitron and his late brother, Felix Guitron Jr., competed on the open show circuit, gaining exposure to the world of professional horsemen and the top trainers of the day. The Guitrons' hometown of Indio, a quiet community in those days, also was the location of a popular show that drew elite horsemen from throughout California. This is where Benny Guitron first met legendary California vaquero Tony Amaral and set his sights on becoming a horseman of similar ability.

After his father's death in 1968, Guitron took the leap toward his goal of being a cowboy and called Amaral, asking for a job. Not too long before, a juvenile Guitron had admired Amaral from afar, and now, as a 20-year-old man, Guitron was taking the first steps to fill the boots he so idolized. In the year that followed, he learned some vaquero trade secrets and found he had a natural hand for starting and training horses in the old Spanish methods. The times then were different, and knowledge didn't come by way of books, videos, or clinics.

"That was probably the most secretive era there ever was. If you wanted to learn something you got up real early in the morning and hoped you caught them doing something," Guitron remarks of horsemen he admired. "Tony helped me a lot, but not the way a trainer does today. He'd be telling you a story as you rode through the hills, and if you were smart enough, you'd figure out he just got done telling you what to do to the horse you were riding. If you didn't get it, he figured that you obviously didn't want it bad enough."

Just eight years later, in 1976, Guitron won his first National Reined Cow Horse Association World Championship Snaffle Bit Futurity title on Kit's Smoke. Guitron went on to win the 1979 NRCHA Bridle Horse Championship and 1979 All-Around Stock-Horse World Championship on this mare. He is the only rider to make the finals of the stock-horse contest every year entered—a total of six times.

Guitron also has been a finalist at every major cow-horse snaffle-bit futurity and is a two-time winner of the NRCHA Snaffle Bit Maturity, as well as being the 1983 NRCHA Hackamore Maturity winner. He holds multiple American Quarter Horse Association world-championship titles, including 2002 Senior Working Cow Horse World Champion, and youth and amateurs under his tutelage have won several world championships. In 2008, Guitron received the highest honor for his contributions to the reined cow-horse industry—induction into the National Reined Cow Horse Association Hall of Fame.

Guitron resides in Merced, Calif., with longtime partner, Paula Diuri, a horse enthusiast in her own right. The horseman openly professes his gratitude for her support, saying, "I owe a lot of my success to that girl."

Throughout his prosperous career, Guitron has surrounded himself with good horsemen, who became not only his mentors, but also his friends. Included among them are Bobby Ingersoll, Matlock Rose, Wayne Havens, and Greg Ward. As for their contributions to his life, Guitron simply says, "I have been so blessed."

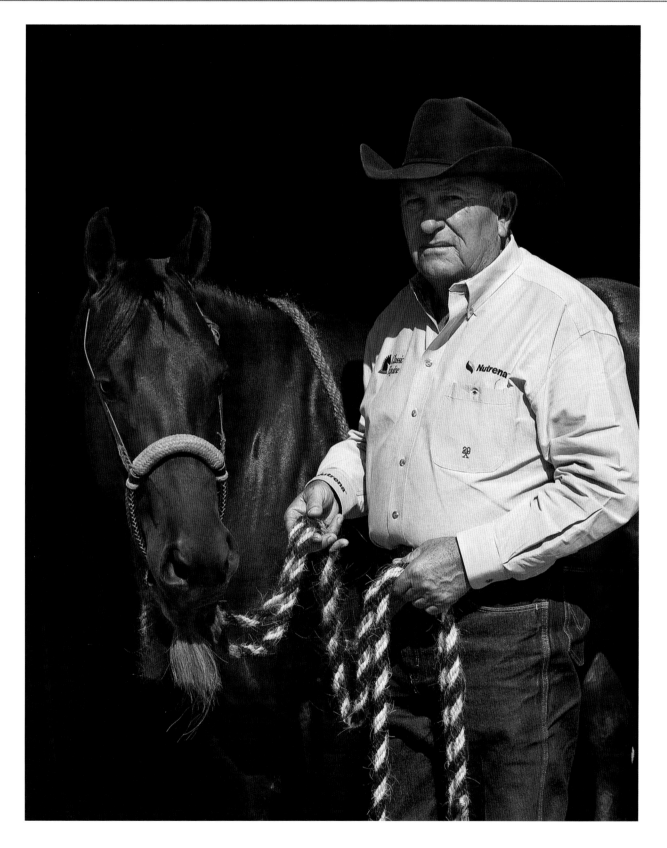

Meet Al

Al Dunning currently trains out of his Almosta Ranch in Scottsdale, Arizona. The father of two, he was born in Chicago, Ill., in 1950 and moved to Arizona at the age of 8. There, the combination of inspiration, good mentors, and hard work paved the way to Dunning's success in the horse industry.

Growing up while watching the television Westerns *Laramie, My Friend Flicka,* and *Fury* fueled a love of horses in the young would-be trainer. Although Dunning didn't take a shine to showing horses until later, he tagged along to shows just to be around the horses while his youngest sister, Denise, competed. Events in Scottsdale offered different venues, where aside from experiencing the usual horse-show culture, Dunning also worked the roping chutes while team ropers rode and spun their loops. Top cowboys, such as Dale Smith, Dean Oliver, and Chuck Shepherd, made remarkable impressions on a young Dunning. He recalls thinking at the time, "Man, that cowboying is really a big deal."

At the tender age of 12, Dunning met Jim Paul, who not only mentored the eager young trainer, but also actually became a father figure. This was the first of several such crucial connections, which became turning points that changed the course of Dunning's path.

Lessons learned under Paul were tough, and nothing came easy. Broncy colts, wild rides, and creative training techniques put young Dunning in precarious situations that most riders today—youth and adult alike—would balk at experiencing. Back in those days, however, a young man did his job as he was told, trying hard to show no fear. Dunning laughs while reminiscing, then adds, "That's just the way it was back then."

Under Paul's guidance, Dunning became a youth champion in every event, from halter to reining and roping, and he often showed as many as six stock horses per class. "I was like a trainer-youth," Dunning says, summarizing his show experience.

Those many good years with Paul opened doors of opportunity for Dunning, and in 1965 he attended his first big show, the Sacramento State Fair. The great hall-of-fame horses and riders he mingled with there further inspired Dunning as a trainer.

"I just followed Jim [Paul] around with my mouth open," Dunning says, and fondly remembers watching Tony Amaral, Don Dodge, Harry Rose, and Jimmy Williams. "I wanted to be like them."

Back then no one specialized as only a reiner, a pleasure rider, or a hunter-jumper competitor in a single event. Great trainers of the day showed the same horses in reining that they used in pleasure and western-riding classes in original, all-around fashion. The broad spectrum of such an environment allowed a young Dunning not only the opportunity to compete in a full array of events, but also to surround himself with fantastic trainers of all disciplines. Big names, such as Red Neal and Harold Farren, played significant roles in Dunning's early development as a horseman. He studied them, along with Ronnie Richards and Mack Linn at the California shows—everything from their clothing to their training techniques. Those images formed in his mind what he wanted to be—a hackamore man.

"I didn't talk much, but I listened," Dunning recalls. "I got to see those guys work, got to see them be tough, kind, all the gamut of stuff, and then I could choose my way."

At 20 years old, while attending Arizona State University, Dunning worked for John Hoyt, whose influence tipped the scales irrevocably. Hoyt's focus on training with a savvy feel for the horse struck a chord with Dunning, cinching his desire to train horses for a living. He recalls that pivotal moment: "I got it; I felt it."

The final turning point in his professional life came one day in class. Sitting before a stack of books, he looked around the room at all the other kids. "They don't know where they're going," Dunning thought to himself, "but I think I know where I'm going. The only thing I'm really good at is training horses."

And that was it. Dunning left school and hung out his shingle as a horse trainer, never looking back. He opened his Almosta Ranch in 1970 and married his wife, Becky, in 1971.

Wins at some of the really big hacka-more events, including Del Mar, the Santa Barbara Flower Show and the Phoenix A to Z Show, where the trainers he idolized were competing, kicked off great success for Dunning. That success continued with American Quarter Horse Association world titles in reining, cutting, working cow horse, and western riding. Dunning also has been a finalist or semi-finalist at every major National Cutting Horse Association event, as well as at the National Reined Cow Horse Association's World's Greatest Horseman contest. Together with his students, Dunning is credited with 32 world-championship and reserve-championship titles.

Additional honors awarded the trainer include being named AQHA's 1996 Professional Horseman of the Year and receiving NCHA's 2003 Zane Schulte Trainer of the Year award, as well as the Monte Roberts Equitarian award in 2004 and numerous other honors. Among the noteworthy horses Dunning has trained and shown was Expensive Hobby, who was inducted into the AQHA Hall of Fame in 2007.

As author of the world-renowned book, *Reining,* Dunning has had an impact on thousands of horse enthusiasts. The knowledge, the passion he shares in his clinics, videos, and lessons has molded not only average students, but also some of today's most successful professional horse trainers.

Dunning's ability to reach people comes from his love of horses and out of respect to the mentors in his own life. Anyone who asks about his greatest influences always hears the names Jim Paul, Don Dodge, and John Hoyt, even though Dunning's list of admirable men

runs long. The horsemen who influenced him and helped him along the way never have been taken for granted but, rather, have been taken to heart. In honor of them all, Dunning says, "They're part of me."

"But most endearing is the vaqueros' protection and love of tradition. Their treasures and heirlooms were not material things, but knowledge, passed down...."

1

History of the Hackamore

The hackamore's past remains somewhat vague and mysterious. Its actual origin is virtually untraceable. *La jaquima*, the hackamore, first made itself known in California when it was brought from northern Mexico in the 1770s during the heyday of the grand cattle empires and the legendary Spanish dons with their vast holdings.

Rawhide braiding already had become a lofty craft, meticulously developed in Tibet centuries before. Outsiders, including invaders in foreign lands, sought the skillful braiding and carried the borrowed braiding methods with them as they moved into other countries.

Braiding Origins

The Moors were one such culture responsible for the spread of rawhide work. An ambitious people of Berber, Arab and black African decent, the Moors hailed from coastal North Africa, and in the year 711 they overwhelmed Spain. Moorish customs, old and new, came to meld with the ways of the newly conquered land, and during this Moorish dominion of Spain, the artistry in braiding techniques furthered significantly.

Likewise, the Spaniards continued the same pattern of carrying customs to a conquered land when they came to Mexico in 1519. Thus, the old technique of rawhide braiding—having traveled from the Orient, modified by cultures along the Mediterranean and fine-tuned by European horsemen—finally appeared on the North American continent.

Shortly after the Spanish conquistadors landed in the Western world, *Hernán Cortés* recognized the wealth of early Mexican civilizations and conquered the Aztec kings who controlled the city of Tenochtitlan. Cortés renamed the site Mexico City, founding the new settlement on top of the Aztec ruins. These Spaniards and their descendants came to own great estates and lived well off Aztec riches and commerce.

The Spanish are credited with the reintroduction of horses to the Americas and, in turn, skilled horsemen and rawhide artisans. The indigenous people

A finely made hackamore is not only an art form, but also "using" gear for working cowboys, trainers and horsemen.

An ancient skill, rawhide braiding traveled from the Orient and into Europe before becoming part of North and South American horse industries.

learned leatherwork and braiding techniques, and a fountain of new life came to the rawhide craft.

Early Californios

With the early explorers, horses and vaqueros trickled into Baja and Alta, lower and upper California, even as far back as the 1600s, but the great Spanish colonization took root in 1769. Authorized by the Spanish government, the aristocratic, blue-blooded dons came north from their holdings in Mexico into the virgin rangelands of the American West, establishing what became known as the Mission Trail. *La Misión San Diego de Alcalá*, also known as the Mission of Saint Didacus of Alcalá, was the first of these old churches founded by Fathers Serra, Palou and Parron near the mouth of the San Diego River.

Expedition leaders guided friars, soldiers, colonists and livestock as far as 500 miles northward, founding 21 missions along the way. For their services to Spain, these settlers received large tracts of land, many of which were 50,000 to 350,000 acres of the unspoiled territory. The wild expanses afforded the ranchers lives of luxury. With grazing lands lush, winters mild and water sources ample, the ranchers' cattle in time multiplied by the thousands.

Spanish cattle of the day were long-horned, rangy, tough brutes that required a good vaquero aboard a solid mount to manage them. Each rancher had his own *caballada*, or band of highly trained saddle horses, and a crew of the finest vaqueros he could hire at his disposal.

During these times of ease and abundance the hackamore took firm root in the cowboy traditions of the early West. Well-to-do land-owners and their vaqueros had bountiful amounts of time to practice and perfect the arts of braiding rawhide and training colts in la jaquima.

Though horse-breaking was a necessity without which the entire system would fail, it was taken to a level beyond mere function. How well a vaquero could break a colt was his calling card as a horseman, and in the stiff competition of the time, earning and keeping a position with the dons was no short order. The use of the hackamore peaked so greatly during this period that it morphed into an art form, as well as a contest for supremacy among the artists. A sense of pride led the flamboyant Californios to make better equipment and to develop better training methods than had ever been used before.

Trade routes, established as early as the mid-1500s, brought ships across the Pacific to the Cape Mendocino area, about 300 miles north of San Francisco, then down the coast of California on their way to Mexico. As the demand for tallow, or beef fat, and hides boomed, commerce developed in ports along the Mission Trail. Ships from New York and Hudson Bay sailed around Cape Horn; others came from Asian countries to trade trinkets, spices, and precious metals for the cattle barons' goods.

Days of the Dons

With the influx of people, the dons' wealth surged to grandiose proportions. During this time, silver-laden saddles made their appearance, aboard which Spanish lords, clad in fine velvets and silks, roped bear, deer, elk, cattle, and wild horses for amusement. The early Americans were amazed, not only by the Spaniards' flagrant extravagance, but also by the Spaniards' skill, hospitality and willingness to share knowledge about ranching, cattle and horses.

During this era the vaqueros incorporated the skill of roping into their everyday cattle work. Tradition shifted from the more primitive methods of their heritage to the finer means of subduing an animal by roping its horns and heels. In earlier times, vaqueros had relied on their ability to run down cattle and immobilize them using a tool called the *media luna*, the half-moon. Just as its name implies, the media luna, or hocking knife, was a crescent-shaped blade extending from an eight- to 10-foot shaft, which was used to slash the thick tendon above a cow's hock. Before the development of the vaqueros' artful roping skills, the hocking knife was the only suitable way for large numbers of cattle to be taken down quickly, simplifying the tasks of slaughtering, removing the hides and harvesting the meat.

"Though horse-breaking was a necessity without which the entire system would fail, it was taken to a level beyond mere function."

As the use of the media luna faded, made obsolete by the long *reata*, a braided rope, the vaqueros garnered fame throughout the world for their *dalle vuelta* method of taking turns or dallying a rope around the saddle horn. Eager Americans took to the style of the handy Californios, birthing the lariat-toting, bandana-wearing cowboy who became the icon of the Old West.

It was an extraordinary time, but just as the high peaks of the Sierra Nevada careen downward to the valleys, such days of prosperity plummeted from their lofty highs into virtual extinction. During the drought of 1862-1864, thousands of cattle and horses died due to vanishing feed and water supplies. The cattle industry was brought to its knees, utterly devastated, and the days of the lavish dons were over.

However, the passion and proficiency of these horsemen remains and certainly flavors early Western history with an air of romance. Continuing fascination with the era is bound to the simplicity of the time and the flair and fervor of its characters. The striving of the wage-earning vaqueros to mirror the elegance of the wealthy lords is admirable and appeals to everyone's sense of pride.

But most endearing is the vaqueros' protection and love of tradition. Their treasures and heirlooms were not material things, but knowledge, passed down their lineage in hands-on lessons with wily broncs, whispered braiding tips around campfires, and even scoldings for imperfections in the work.

The hackamore can be both a tool for a great horseman and a finely crafted masterpiece.

These gifts, held sacrosanct within families of the great early California horsemen, still are held dear by the few modern vaqueros who keep the spirit and tradition alive.

Preparing the Hide

Few seldom recognize what a tremendous labor of love the hackamore portrays in its composition alone. The very nature of this time-consuming creation poetically foretells of the training theories that must be honored once the hackamore is seated on a horse's nose. A beautiful concept reveals itself when one examines the patient process and steady poise of the braider's hand—a concept that directly mirrors the compassionate, dedicated practice of building a hackamore horse.

In keeping with the old traditions, modern-day rawhide braiders still use the methods of the vaquero braiders gone before them. Their craft requires hours of preparation to bring raw materials into usable form for such necessities as 80-foot braided reatas, hackamores and headstalls. Back in the time of the vaqueros, *reateros*, or reata makers, considered such work part of their everyday toil as cattlemen.

On long drives and roundups, steers butchered to feed the crew provided the materials for the vaquero's side-job as a reata maker. Hides of slaughtered cattle were removed with care and stretched over boards, staked by wooden pegs in a suspended fashion to allow air circulation beneath. Gunnysacks

"Since I got hurt and couldn't cowboy anymore, I started braiding," said craftsman Don Brown. "But you've got to like braiding an awful lot to do it."

often were used to cover the pegged skins, protecting them from the ravishing effects of the sun.

Fresh steer hides remained pegged-out in the shade until they were dry enough for the hair to be scraped from the hides. Once dried and hair-free, the vaquero's cowhides could be rolled and stored in the chuck wagon, then tempered and cut another day.

Another method of hair removal was to throw a hide into a stream, anchoring it down to soak. About the third day, just as the hide started to smell a little tainted, it was removed from the water, and the hair slicked off the flesh with ease. If a hide was left too long in the water, however, decay set in, ruining the hide altogether.

Today braiders prefer the elbow-grease method of scraping a hide, hour after hour, to the soaking method although some do use lye to remove the hair. However, if not monitored properly and neutralized correctly, lye can burn a hide and destroy the rawhide's elasticity. It is, therefore, the opinion of many rawhide artisans that the more natural, though less efficient, method of scraping is the means of the purist, who takes greatest care in the quality of his finished products.

Salt-cured hides did not find favor with many reateros, who used other family recipes kept as trade secrets within their tightly bound groups. Tempering a hide was achieved by soaking it in water until the hide took on a firm, plastic-like feel. It was known and understood then, just as it is today, that the preparatory process, if rushed or incomplete, leaves fluids and blood in the material that cause decomposition in the rawhide. So, it is only after these initial stages of preparation have been fulfilled and the hide trimmed of blemishes and weak areas, such as the belly, neck and flank, that the hide finally can be considered ready for cutting.

Cutting and Beveling

The painstaking task of cutting a hide has changed little through the course of time. Just as in days of old, the job requires a reatero to work in a spiral, slicing a single, long strip, approximately 1½ to 2 inches wide, from the hide. The strip is then refined and made uniform by splitting the excess off the flesh-side. Next, the strip must be cut down into four, six or eight strands, leaving workable ½- to ⅛-inch strips, ready for beveling.

Beveling the grain-side edges of the rawhide strings ensures that the finished product remains smooth under the rigors of everyday work, as well as the moisture of sweat and the elements. Without this tedious beveling process, some edges likely curl into sharp imperfections, absolutely unacceptable in quality

Although some old-time draw gauges might have been a bit more crudely made than the one shown, the tool continues to hold a place in the braider's craft.

This string cutter can be used to both bevel and smooth the edges of rawhide strings.

equipment. These rough edges are removed with ultimate delicacy and exactitude, with the aid of a gauge, which in the old days was made from a notched piece of wood and sharp knife.

Braiding Considerations

Only after meticulous beveling are the rawhide strands ready for braiding reatas, hackamores and other vaquero gear. Glycerin, lanolin, beeswax and rawhide creams are some of the products braiders use to soften the leather for braiding, though certain preferences and techniques are kept hushed. Some artisans seal their finished braid work in the old manner, by rubbing it with cold beef liver. This process thwarts minute bugs, which otherwise can infiltrate the braid, eating it from the inside out.

In addition to such age-old techniques, many of the old-time reatero's tools are still in use today, with little change. The flesher, for example, is a clever, though simple, tool through which rawhide strands are pulled to achieve the desired thickness. Awls, metal mallets, punches, and needles are other traditional staples of the braider's workbench, and even with modern conveniences, many traditionalists prefer handmade tools similar to

those used by their predecessors. In the times of the vaquero braiders, crude tools had to be kept as sharp as possible for precise tasks, and improvising was inevitable. The rustic braiders were adept and inventive, perfecting their skills amid a taxing lifestyle.

As the craft of braiding blossomed into an art form, braiders learned the importance of hide selection. Hides from cattle of particular ages, weights, breeds, and colors became recognized for specific properties, as well as the type of project for which a particular type of hide found the most favor. Light calfskin, for example, which turned out a less robust strand than the sturdy, elastic hide of an older animal, was better suited for decorative buttons and fine detail work. A hide from a thinner animal with some age and size was chosen for fashioning a reata or other gear that required greater integrity to handle the demands of the intended workload.

Increasingly sophisticated braiding techniques flourished, made manifest in interwoven patterns in an array of shades and colors. Although a simple braid could be completed in a half-day's time, extravagant work could require multiple days, the maker toiling at a higher level of tedium. Consequently, the early vaquero displayed his equipment proudly aboard his finely trained mount—further testament to the diligence and skill of his hands.

A longtime braider's tools reflect both quality and use.

2

Hackamores and Mecates

The vaquero's hackamore comprises a headstall, or hanger, the mecate rein, and a braided nosepiece, commonly referred to as the bosal. Traditionally, however, this term was not used in the sense it is today. In Spanish, *bozal* literally means "muzzle" and originally referenced only the pencil bosal, or the small *bosalito* worn under the bridle in the hackamore horseman's two-rein setup.

Although modern horsemen have come to use the terms "hackamore" and "bosal" interchangeably, traditional hackamore men frown upon this. In historical context, bosal designates nosepieces ¼- to ⅜-inch in diameter, and all other sizes from ½-inch and upward are known as hackamores. In keeping with tradition, here, all nosepieces are referred to as hackamores except for the bosalito, or pencil bosal.

A complex creation, in both design and methodology, the hackamore has been developed through the centuries to meet the needs of trainers and horses. Ask any hackamore man and he says that for proper function the hackamore must have life to it—a certain spring and snap. That life is what gives the quick, concise cue-and-release necessary for hackamore training.

Hackamore Construction

The life in a hackamore comes from its core. Cores are made of different materials although a good rawhide core often is preferred over other types, such as an old length of reata or mecate. A rawhide core produces the desirable feel and life, whereas other braided cores with less life and snap are slower to affect the horse.

Yet another element that requires patience in the braider's routine work, a core must be made and left to dry for days, even weeks, to ensure a good finished product that doesn't mold and break down. Braiders create either smooth rawhide cores or twisted cores, depending on personal preference. A twisted core is wrapped until the rawhide is flush between the ridges before the next layer is applied.

Hackamores are made in different diameters for different purposes and also come in a variety of braid plaits, or strand counts. A typical work hackamore can vary from a rugged eight-plait to a more refined 12-plait braid; the simpler the braid, the faster it can be made. A decent braider can make an eight-plait hackamore in three hours, aside from the

No matter how different the braiding, colors, craftsmanship or materials, all hackamores have the same general construction features.

The four primary parts of a hackamore are the heel knot, cheeks, side buttons and nose button.

initial making of the core and strands. More elaborate braids, such as 24- and 32-plaits, take considerably longer and demand that a braider take breaks throughout the process to relieve stress. The higher the plait, the more days the braider spends although the actual time frame depends strictly on the individual.

The hackamore consists of four basic parts—heel knot, cheeks, side buttons, and nose button. The heel knot is the base, on top of which the mecate is tied, and commonly is round in shape or tapered in a variation called the pineapple knot. The pear-shaped heel knot is longer in length than its more circular counterpart and also is widely used, but other variations do exist. Heel knots are as individual as the braiders who make them and come in an array of shapes and sizes; some are larger, others more slight, yet others more tapered or even semi-square in shape.

The nose button, also called the *impalme*, is the raised, rounded portion that goes

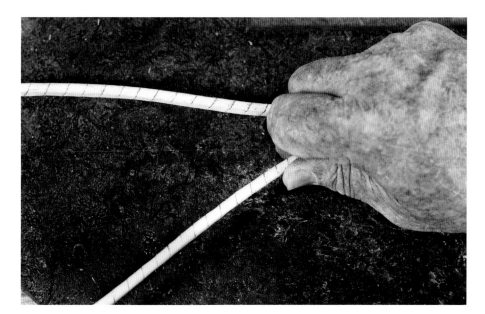

Although a rawhide core is time-consuming to make, which contributes to the cost, most horsemen think this type core produces better results than cores made of other materials.

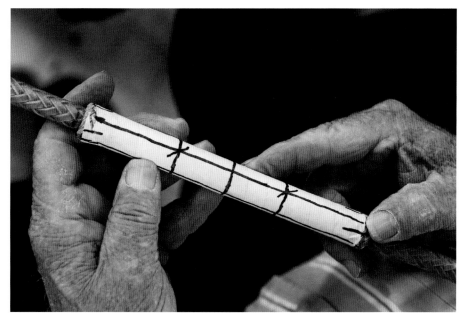

The build-up on this nose button ultimately will be part of a ½-inch, 12-strand hackamore.

across the bridge of the horse's nose. Typically 7½ inches wide, the nose button is the crucial balance point of the hackamore on the horse's face. Thicker than the cheeks of the hackamore, the nose button is built up by a succession of braids and wraps until the desired size and shape are achieved. A poorly made nose button, or one of rough, uneven braid, does not convey the intended messages to the horse's sensitive nose and likely can break his skin.

The cheeks are the sides of the hackamore, also known as the shanks. Typically, the cheek braid of a hackamore is made with fewer plaits than the nose button, which creates an eye-pleasing contrast. For example, a 12-plait cheek typically carries a 16-plait nosepiece, while the 16-plait cheek is crowned by a 24-plait nose. A showy 24-plait cheek is adorned by 32-plait nose button, and so on. Some show hackamores can be so extravagant in detail as to have the mind-bending 40-plait braid. The mastery of such a delicate braid is awe-inspiring. There is, however, much more to this design than mere fashion. The more intricate the braid, the smoother its finish and softer the hackamore is on the horse's nose. This is why it's common to see a higher-plait nose button than cheeks—to prevent skinning the horse's nose while giving a little more stern command to his jaw line than to his nose.

Hackamore Artistry

Each braider knows when and where to lay colored strands into a braid to create vivid patterns and complex designs. He works from his ingenuity, without stencil or pattern to follow, even on the most intricate of motifs. Hides of different cattle breeds provide the variations in strand color, ranging from creamy white to caramel, all the way to dark amber. Textile dyes also can be used to make the bold reds and other hues favored by some braiders; however, if not

Hackamore strand colors vary with the colors of the cowhides used, just as color in a mecate results from the horsehair used to make it.

cured properly, artificial dyes can bleed and discolor the natural rawhide. Traditional artisans and braiders frown on such a flaw. Pride in their rawhide craft requires that their work is not only functional, but also symmetrical and correct in both structure and design, or it is unacceptable.

An artisan of particular, indisputable influence on rawhide braiding was the late Luis Ortega. His legacy lives on in the expectations of quality and artistry associated with the modern hackamore and the whole of the rawhide trade. Ortega took the modest, functional braid work of the old Californios and cultivated it into a museum-worthy art form. His superior braiding laid the foundation for the other great braiders to follow, and certainly cinched the hackamore's survival in the face of the vaquero's extinction.

Ernie Morris, another influential braider, artist and horseman, also can be credited for the braiding tradition's survival. He has helped to maintain the bridge between the present and the old days so that the history and skills not come asunder. Tom Kerr and Tony Araujo also hold honorable seats in the lineage of great braiders, having set the stage for such modern braiders as Don Brown and Steve Guitron to continue the craft. In so many ways, the hackamore has been carried, as if slung over the shoulders of men such as these, from the humblest beginnings down a long road through changing times.

The Hackamore Blueprint

In the old days most hackamores were 12 inches in length, measured from the inside of the nose button to the heel knot. The blood of the Roman-nosed Spanish Barb ran thick in the early Californios' horses and perpetuated stock of robust stature and spirit. Compared to small-muzzled modern equines, horses of that time were rawboned, jugheaded hombres of little refinement. They simply couldn't fit into the downsized, 10½- to 11-inch hackamores in use today.

Though necessity has conjured modifications to the hackamore's original design, the basic blueprint remains unchanged in regard to mechanics and equine physiology. The hackamore works by communicating cues from rider to mount by way of the nerves in the boney structures of the horse's muzzle and jaw. Coarse-nosed and dish-faced horses alike share a common nerve structure.

The horsehair cheeks of this hackamore create a different feel to a horse than cheeks braided of rawhide, a difference a horseman considers when selecting his training gear.

Thickness of flesh and bone, however, do play a role in a horse's sensitivity, and, therefore, some horses do give more readily to the hackamore than others.

The trigeminal nerve, or fifth cranial nerve, is the nerve responsible for sensation in the horse's face. Another nerve, the infraorbital, is a branch of the maxillary nerve, and is one of the superhighways of sensation throughout the nasal structure. The mandibular labial nerve, located in the mandible or jaw of the horse, is a main carrier of information from his chin and lower-muzzle region back to the brain. A multitude of peripheral nerves branch from these to form a spider web of sensors throughout the subcutaneous layers to the horse's outermost skin. Even the long guard hairs of the horse's soft-skinned muzzle are a part of the brilliant nervous

Although all hackamores seem to look alike, the diameter of each affects its intended purpose.

system, sending clues about the environment that can help him maneuver safely in the dark. It is through these many nerves and their branches that the hackamore is able to communicate cues from the rider's hands to the horse's mind, which the horse translates, through his rider's teaching, into action with the rest of his body.

Training Considerations

The sensitivity of the horse's head structures demands compassion, empathy, and savvy in training. Bad hands can ruin a hackamore horse in less time than it takes the rawhide braider to build the hackamore in the first place. To develop a good horse, a rider must understand the hackamore's movement on the horse's nose—how first the nose button rolls on his nasal bones, followed by the hackamore cheeks contacting the jawbone.

Just as the hackamore must have life to it, so must the trainer's hands have life. In form and function, the hackamore is designed to give and release, never to be pulled on by dead, heavy hands. In the vaqueros' time an esteemed horseman was considered to be only as good as his tack, but that theory sprang from a deeper truth—a horseman is only as good as his understanding of his tack and its crucial importance to the horse.

Because of the hackamore's leverage, a green horse easily can be confused. It is common for him to misconstrue the rider's cue for lateral bend with a request for vertical flexion from the poll and tucking his

Another consideration when selecting a hackamore is an individual horse's sensitivity, which might mean using headgear with rope cheeks.

nose. This phase of the horse's learning is of infinite importance and cannot be rushed. By training with empathy and knowledge, a good hand gives the horse time to think, process and respond, conditioning him in time to the desired task.

This patient approach also is key to avoid hurting, numbing or frightening the developing hackamore horse. Putting him into a large, stiff hackamore with too much bite can prove a devastating mistake. Likewise, starting a horse in a pencil bosal, intended for use further along in his training, can be a foolish enterprise.

The ⅝-inch hackamore is the size preferred for starting colts, though a ¾-inch hackamore also can be used. Either of these sizes affords good feel to the horse, and regardless of size, the hackamore should have a flexible, snappy core. It is best to avoid starting a green hackamore horse in a hackamore with a heavy, stiff core that might scare or sore him. Back in the old days, the big-boned, thick-hided horses of the time could be put into large, stiff hackamores without the repercussions one might experience with the soft-skinned horses of today.

As a horse progresses in training, he can be moved into a smaller ½-inch hackamore, which prepares him for the light ⅜- and ¼-inch bosalitos placed under the bridle for guidance when a horse transitions to working solely with the traditional spade bit. This phase of training, referred to as the two-rein, is the introductory period for using a solid bit in the horse's virgin mouth. He carries the bosalito and bridle together, and is guided by two sets of reins—the hackamore reins to which he is accustomed and the new reins connected to the bit.

Permanent teeth begin erupting in the equine mouth at 2½ years of age, which corresponds with the time that most colts are started. Second and third incisors come in from 3½ to 4½ years, and the adult mouth is finally complete by age 5, with the horse's canine or bridle teeth.

The lightweight bosalito is used under the bridle when a horse is in the two-rein phase of training and is being introduced to a solid bit.

However, much of today's modern training procedure is based on the snaffle-to-bridle method, which keeps a bit in the horse's mouth throughout his career under saddle. When responding to pressure from a bit in the already-inflamed tissues of his young mouth, a horse can learn to fight the snaffle and its variations, and damage his sensitive bars, cheeks and tongue. Not only are the tissues and nerve structures bruised and disrupted, but the horse's mind and thought process alike. His response to pain can be expressed by gapping his mouth, chomping the bridle, pinning his ears, flashing his tail and often fighting hard to resist training. Riding a horse with a bit through this phase of his growth can lead to forceful training methods and sometimes permanent damage to his mouth and mind.

The hackamore method takes the bit out of a young horse's changing, sensitive mouth, and it is believed that the horse is better for it when the time of the two-rein comes around. Hackamore enthusiasts boastfully consider an aged hackamore horse, now ready for the two-rein, to have a pristine mouth, free from bruises, scars, and bad habits.

> **"Hackamore enthusiasts boastfully consider an aged hackamore horse, now ready for the two-rein, to have a pristine mouth, free from bruises, scars, and bad habits."**

The Mecate

The traditional reins of the hackamore are called the mecate, which literally means "rope" in Spanish. In regard to reins, a mecate is typically a natural fiber rope made from horse mane or tail hair although other natural fibers and synthetics are common. Historically, these types of ropes have been made from various plant and animal sources for different purposes. As far back as 200 BC, the Mesoamerican people of Teotihuacan used the maguey, or agave, plant's long fibers

Mecates are available in a variety of designs and colors, and softer mane hair generally is preferred to more coarse tail hair.

to build ropes and weave fabrics. Their style of twisting the fibers, rather than braiding them, has been improved through the centuries, but is still in use today.

Though known as braiders, mecate makers actually twist the mane hair, usually 6 to 8 inches long, to create the strands necessary for building the traditional rein. The braider feeds fibers from a gunny sack onto a spinning hook until the desired thickness and length of the strand are achieved. This time-consuming process demands both hours and patience.

A typical mecate consists of three twisted strands, each 66 feet in length, which are then twisted together to make the standard 22-foot mecate rein for the hackamore. The diameters

of the mecate correspond to the sizes of the hackamore—a ¾-inch mecate is tied on a ¾-inch hackamore, and a ¼-inch mecate is tied on the bosalito for the two-rein setup.

Tail hair also is used in mecates, but is much coarser than mane hair and far harsher on the rider's hands. Tail hair is not favored above the gentler, more pliable mane hair reins, though some infer that the prickly tail hair has benefits when it comes to neck-reining, as the coarse tail hair encourages a horse to move away from the rein.

Mohair, or goat hair, also is used in making the mecate, and even alpaca fibers. Alpaca mecates are soft and inviting to the touch, though braiders say that the alpaca fiber, due to its silky constitution, is far more challenging to work. Many synthetic mecates are on the market today, often made from yacht cord with leather buttons added by the braider.

Though some old-fashioned horsemen hold true to the original, or natural, fibers and even chastise others for the use of synthetics, there is room to argue manmade fibers into the accepted tradition. Old-time cowboys relied on nature's provision for materials to build their equipment, and no part of the task came easily. Had such a luxury as yacht cord been afforded them, they likely would have been thrilled with the ease of the sturdy, low-maintenance product. Personal preference is really of greatest importance in the end, as the equipment must have the right feel in the rider's hands.

Chestnut, black, brown, flaxen, gray and white are some of the natural colors that horsehair fibers offer the braider when designing patterns in the mecate rein. As with the rawhide braider, a mecate maker knows when to lay color into the weave to create the motif in his mind.

Interestingly, however, rawhide braiders and mecate braiders are, metaphorically, horses of a different color. Both are artists, connected by trade, history, and necessity, but rarely do both crafts materialize in the hands of a single craftsman. There are only a few rawhide braiders who braid mecates, and a few mecate braiders who braid rawhide. Imagine a small village in a simpler time, which was home to a family of leather workers, and another that was home to a line of fiber workers. Each family protected and perpetuated the craft of their group's specific work, relying on basic principles of supply and demand to meet their needs. Trade and commerce arose from the monopoly these tradesmen held over their individual crafts, with each relying on the other.

Perhaps a shadow of that way of life continues in a dormant way. Tight-lipped

For many contemporary horsemen, mecates made of low-maintenance, manmade fibers have proven acceptable alternatives to horsehair mecates.

traditional braiders and makers hold sacred the techniques their predecessors have bestowed upon them. Although modern times have changed the equation drastically, it is still plausible that the sense of importance today's braiders feel is an emotion of old, passed down from a time when the craft was more than a skilled trade, but a means of sustenance and the key to survival.

"The placement of the reins, higher or lower on the heel knot, lends to the lateral- or vertical-flexion results you can achieve when riding."

3
Tying the Mecate

There are several different methods of tying the mecate, each with a unique theory behind the method. The placement of the loop rein, higher or lower on the heel knot, lends to the lateral- or vertical-flexion results you can achieve when riding your horse.

A higher rein-set, with the rein positioned a couple wraps up from the heel knot, produces more lateral, side-to-side flexion for the green hackamore horse than does a rein set lower on the heel knot. Reins placed close to the heel knot induce greater vertical bend by encouraging the horse to tuck in his nose as a result of poll flexion. Other variations in tying a mecate can include the position of the lead rope alongside the heel knot and rein, as well as the number of wraps taken around the hackamore, which aids in sizing the hackamore and affects the weight of it.

Tying Method One
This first method of tying a mecate results in a high rein-set with the lead rope extending from the front of the tie.

No matter which method for tying a mecate you prefer, each method is a step-by-step process that becomes easy to do with practice.

When tying a mecate, rein placement, the position of the lead and the number of wraps taken vary, depending on the tying method used, and can affect not only how the hackamore fits a horse, but also how the horse responds.

To begin, hold the heel knot with the hanger on top, as if the hackamore was on a horse. Here, the hanger has been hung over a saddle horn. Place the tassel end of the mecate down through the V created by the hackamore cheeks and leave a couple inches of the mecate dangling below the heel knot.

Start wrapping the mecate around the right cheek, as shown, before placing one complete wrap on top of the other, proceeding from the heel knot toward the nose button.

Usually two wraps are sufficient for an average-sized horse. A large-muzzled horse might require only one wrap, and a fine-muzzled horse could require three. The length of your hackamore also helps determine how many wraps you need—more for a longer hackamore, fewer for a shorter one.

Next, pull a loop from the mecate through the V to form the rein. A general rule of thumb: A wingspan-length of rein, from fingertip to fingertip, is appropriate.

Take care to ensure that the mecate loop rein is straight and smooth, not twisted or kinked, before you secure the rein with another wrap.

Complete the final step by slipping the mecate tail in between the reins and the final wrap, as shown.

Then pull the mecate knot snug around the hackamore cheeks and heel knot.

With this tying method the loop rein sits just below the lead rope. Now open the hackamore by taking a hold of the cheeks and pulling them apart near the mecate.

Tying Method Two

The second mecate-tying method illustrates a lower rein set with the lead rope extending from the back of the hackamore and alongside the loop rein, the tying style Benny Guitron favors. His use of the shorter 10- to 10½-inch hackamore enables him to make fewer wraps and still achieve the correct fit.

As before, place the tassel end of the mecate down through the V, leaving a couple inches dangling below the heel knot, and bring the mecate over the right cheek.

Start your first wrap, but before completing it, pull your rein loop through the V, as shown.

Guitron then prefers to cross the loop rein as that can reduce the risk of the rein feeding through this setup, which has fewer wraps.

Make one or two wraps on top of the crossed rein to achieve the appropriate fit for your horse's muzzle.

Complete the final wrap by bringing the mecate tail from the right side, through the V and beneath the final wrap, so it extends through the back of your hackamore, next to the rein.

The lead rope then rests to the side of the loop rein, as shown here from the tassel side. When the hackamore is on your horse, with the tassel hanging down, the lead is on your horse's near side.

Pull everything snug, but not so snug that the hackamore becomes narrow or tight against your horse's lower jaw. As before, open your hackamore by pulling the cheeks apart near the mecate.

Tying Method Three

This third procedure demonstrates Al Dunning's tying method, with the lead rope resting between the reins. Dunning prefers the longer 11- to 11½-inch hackamore used with more wraps to the shorter hackamore Guitron prefers. You still can use this third way to tie a mecate on a shorter hackamore by simply reducing the number of wraps you take around the cheeks.

Begin by placing the tassel end of the mecate down through the V before starting your wraps.

Make your wraps around the cheeks and then pull your rein loop from the front of the hackamore through the V and under the wrap.

As previously suggested, an arm-span is a general guideline for setting the length of the rein.

Continue making consecutive, smooth wraps around the cheeks until the hackamore is appropriately sized for your horse. A long hackamore might require three wraps above the reins. Make your final pass around the right cheek of the hackamore and bring the mecate tail through the loop to rest between the reins.

Ensure that all the wraps are neatly tucked down close to one another as you pull the mecate snug to secure the tie.

After tying the mecate, don't forget to open the hackamore by taking hold of the cheeks near the mecate and pulling them apart.

Consider the Horse

It should be noted that with any tying method, a good horseman analyzes not only his horse's facial size and structure, but also his needs throughout the course of training. A green horse learning to give laterally benefits from the higher rein-set and a looser hackamore that doesn't bite into his jaw as much as a tighter hackamore. As the horse's training advances, the rein can be lowered for more vertical control, and the mecate knot again tightened.

It is important to remember that every horse is an individual. Although one hackamore setup works superbly on one animal,

the same setup might work differently for another horse. Vigilance is of the utmost sig-

"As the horse's training advances, the rein can be lowered for more vertical control, and the mecate knot again tightened."

nificance. Keep an analytical focus on your horse's reactions and progress; doing so helps you understand his needs so you can make modifications accordingly.

"If somebody came up to me and said, 'You can have your choices of the snaffle, half-breed, spade bit, or the hackamore, but you're only going to get one to ride in from now on,' I would certainly take the hackamore over all of them."

—Jim Paul

4

Training in the Hackamore

On a Sunday morning, not too terribly long ago, a weatherworn cowhand buffed the trail dust off his everyday work saddle. The rough country had left a few scratches on the cannon bones of his sun-bleached partner, and the cowboy used a stiff-bristled brush to flick off the scabs that were ready to peel. Downed fences had been mended, sick calves doctored and the branding done. With a pat on the stout bay's neck, a soft smile touched the corners of the cowboy's mouth.

Though he'd managed to gentle the gelding, initially a striking bronc, to accept the saddle and a lariat swung from his back, the heart of a wild horse still was inside. But, after all the miles he and the cowboy had logged together, this round-rumped, bright-eyed horse had learned to use his prowess in partnership. Never outrun by cattle in the hills, nor outmaneuvered in the sorting pen, the bay, from a hard run, could set up and roll hard over his hocks, springing completely around in the other direction, to dominate the gnarliest of cattle.

The show in town would gather ranch hands from different counties, even the foreman of the neighboring outfit and that fancy sorrel he rode. A glimmer of admiration lit the cowboy's eyes as he compared his bay to the fast-footed sorrel. With pride, the cowboy ran a red handkerchief over the small white spot on the bay's forehead. This bay horse was the best working horse around, and today the cowboy would wager his hard-earned dollar to prove it.

Practical Application

This humble beginning spurred the western show horse into being, yet the simplistic, functional beauty in that truth often is forgotten. Now in an age when horses under lights and blankets live in box stalls, it seems that everyone has lost sight of the stony trails leading the industry to this point. However, beneath

The soft feel revered by a hackamore horseman carries into the bridle as the horse progresses in his training.

almost every stock-horse event lies the sweat of a long day's work and dusty miles of fence line across bad ground.

The reining horse's stops, rollbacks, and spins once were more than fancy footwork; they were the means of outsmarting and out-stepping cattle that didn't always follow the herd. The western rider's lead change owes its heritage to the cowboy's need to be on lead when circling a calf in either direction, and to

> ## "For the working horse of yesteryear, all the demands the rider placed on a horse made sense in a form-to-function way, for he had a task-oriented job..."

the handiness of his mount and his ability to accommodate by changing lead on the fly. All these components long have been the staples of ranch life, the tools of the trade that make tough jobs easier than they otherwise might be.

Ever proud of their lifework, the cow-boys came from the hills into town, each to show that his mount was better than the rest. However, horses today work to show, while the horse of old showed how well he worked.

Training Psychology

In many ways modern horses have life easier than did their ancestors. Hoof-care, dentistry, pristine shelters, and excellent feed and supplementation are but a few of the perks for a horse of the present era. However, when it comes to the psychology of training, it is arguable that the hardworking, old-time ranch horse had it better than the show horse of today.

Most colts nowadays are enclosed in four-walled environments and asked to move in ways they never would at liberty. They're told to trot or lope, lap after lap, going nowhere and with no purpose. Riders teach horses to side-pass, arc and flex, and to turn around and around, and try to train through any obstinacy as it arises. Although all horses in the pro-cess of becoming broke sometimes challenge training, modern riders face many struggles

rooted in this plain fact—the horse today sees no apparent reason for his movements other than that his rider requires him to do so.

For the working horse of yesteryear, all the demands the rider placed on a horse made sense in a form-to-function way, for he had a task-oriented job to which every maneu-ver related. As soon as a colt was accepting of a rider aboard, the colt was out on the range for a long day's work. He was lined-out toward a destination and along the way learned to steer left and right, and to stop and back while controlling cattle. The everyday task of navigating a sage-covered hillside offered a tremendous training session for the green mount. He learned to neck-rein while working his way through the brush; every rock in the way became another opportunity for his rider to teach the colt proper steering. In a timely fashion, the horse came to associate the rider's cues with a job, which gave the colt a purpose, a reason to comply.

In contemplating the mentality of such a horse's equine counterparts today and the demands placed on them, a sense of compassion and empathy is surely due contemporary horses. Most modern horse trainers never have an opportunity to train in a working-ranch environment. With horses nowadays confined to arenas, it is imperative that each horse's learning process be made as stress-free as possible; an environment must be cultivated that allows him to relate his rider's demands to a reason and to receive a reward for his compliance.

Why the Hackamore

With the vast majority of trainers now-adays implementing the snaffle-to-bridle method, it's almost forgotten what prece-dence the hackamore once held in the horse industry. Many people today wonder why they would put their horses in the hacka-more at all. However, by design, the snaffle bit enables a horse to become heavy in hand and lay into the bit. Envision a racehorse—the desire is that he be bold and get into the jockey's grip. But in the western horse school of thought, the coveted lightness in a riding horse requires that he balance himself, stay-ing off the rider's hands and never leaning into pressure.

Stretch a scarf or bandana across the table. Then take the end of the bandana in your fingers, and pull it toward you—this represents the lightness and feel of a properly trained hackamore horse. As your hand closes around the mecate and draws the rein around, your horse follows with no resistance—only absolute softness. This is the feel so revered by the hackamore man and a softness that carries into the bridle as the horse progresses in his work. To achieve such willingness without force takes more than an average trainer; it takes a student of the art.

Before the age of futurities, it was commonplace for all western horses to be ridden in the hackamore. It made sense to keep a bit out of a young horse's changing mouth, preserving his bars, pallet, and chin groove for the bridle. It was understood in those days that training required time to take effect. Horses weren't forced through cram courses, with trainers feeling pressured to make horses perform by predetermined show dates. Back then, a horse simply learned what he learned when he learned it, and his comprehension and retention were understood to be no more coercible than the weather.

No two horses respond to training at the same pace; some soak up their educations as if they're sponges while others fight or fail to grasp the concepts for a time. With many gimmicks on the market today to help force horses into submission, patience has taken a backseat in many programs. No matter how many gimmicks might be used, not one is a substitute for a solid training foundation. Just as a house built on muddy slope eventually slides down an embankment, a horse rushed into performance can last only so long. Taking the time the horse needs and showing him consistency in command, consequence, and reward might be a slower process, but in the end makes a better broke horse than does hurrying a horse to perform. The purpose of the hackamore, then, is to set the stage for a bridle, and when done correctly, makes the transition easy.

As you move ahead into the techniques of hackamore training, be mindful of the underlying theories and embark on each training session with an analytical, yet compassionate and empathetic eye.

Fitting the Hackamore

The setup and fit of the hackamore is as important to the training process as hide selection is to the braider's work. With the same thoughtfulness the rawhide artisan uses

in choosing the proper hide for each braid, so must the hackamore man ensure that the hackamore and the horse are correctly matched in order to turn out a fine result. Even the best braiding technique in the world cannot manufacture a quality hackamore from the wrong materials, and the same is true of using ill-fitting equipment to train a hackamore horse.

Fitting a hackamore to the structure and skin of each animal is crucial, as is knowing when it's time to change or modify a horse's headgear. Variations in the coarseness or softness of the hackamore in use should change with the natural ebb and flow of training. A savvy trainer doesn't have one favorite hackamore, but rather chooses the one favorable to the horse he's about to ride.

The standard fit of a hackamore places the nose button approximately halfway between the eyes and muzzle of the horse, but variations in skull conformation can have an impact on placement. On a long-muzzled horse with high-set eyes, for example, the hackamore might end up appearing to be lower on his nose than a hackamore appears on the head of a horse more balanced and proportionate in his build.

Ensure proper placement of the hackamore by feeling the structure of the bridge of your horse's nose; carefully note where the bone ends and ties into the cartilage and soft tissue of the muzzle. The hackamore should not rest so low that it is near this area, where the bridge and muzzle converge. At rest, the hackamore should sit on the bridge, away from the nostrils and muzzle, with the heel knot and mecate wraps resting at the chin. If the heel knot isn't touching the horse's chin when the reins are slack, the hackamore is too high and too tight to function properly.

An easy way to size the hanger of the hackamore is to place your right hand atop your horse's poll and lift out the hanger slack with your thumb until the correct fit is achieved. Note the length of adjustment necessary, so you then can remove that amount of slack and rehitch the hanger.

Although correct fit is of utmost relevance in all circumstances, explore different theories and methods to try and find the right setup for your individual horse. When selecting an appropriately sized hackamore for your horse, there are two schools of thought from which to choose.

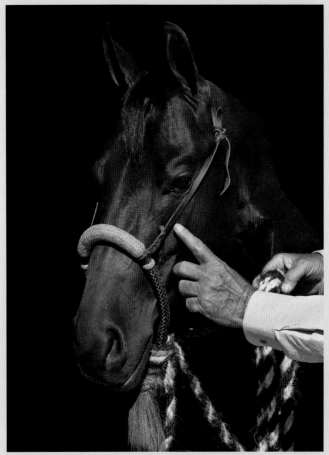

Generally, the nose button rests halfway between a horse's eyes and his muzzle.

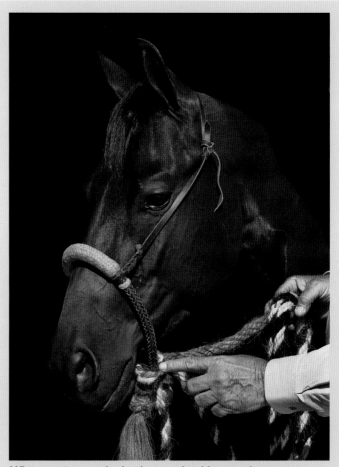

When not in use, the hackamore heel knot and mecate wraps rest at the horse's chin.

Benny Guitron prefers the shorter 10- to 10½- inch hackamore, as he thinks it better fits smaller, modern horses. With fewer wraps of the mecate necessary on the heel knot, Guitron believes that such a hackamore does not move or bounce excessively, which causes irritation that can confuse a horse about signals coming from the rider.

Al Dunning, on the other hand, chooses a little longer hackamore, 11- to 11½-inches, which enables him to put a couple more mecate wraps above the knot. His theory is that the additional length and wraps allow the hackamore to give a more distinct signal to the horse and to fall away from the horse faster than is otherwise possible.

Both trainers favor the shorter 6½- to 7½ -inch nose button that corresponds with the nerve structures alongside the bridge of a horse's nose. Longer nose buttons gained popularity due to an interest in the horses' comfort, but arguably are not as well-aligned

with the desired pressure points as shorter nose buttons are. If the hackamore hanger rides too near the eyes of a particular horse, a simple string around the jowl can be used to alleviate that concern without compromising the proper feel and signal the short nose button offers the horse.

When using either a long or short hackamore, a good horseman must have enough sense to pick up on what a particular horse needs. Aside from proper fit, each mount can have individual preferences, with some preferring a little more movement from the hackamore and others less. Having a variety of sizes and styles of hackamores enables an attentive trainer to accommodate any horse throughout the training process.

A hackamore with a ⅝-inch diameter is considered the most common for introducing this headgear to a green horse, and a hackamore with a good, lively core with spring and snap is the best. A stiff core has more bite

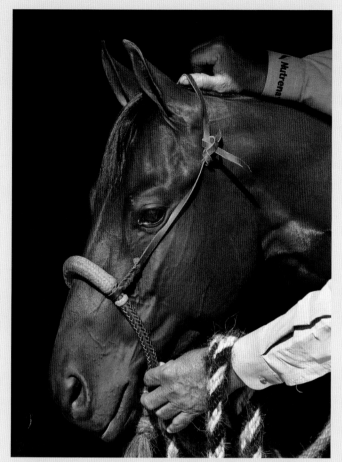

Using a thumb at a horse's poll makes it easy to size the hackamore hanger.

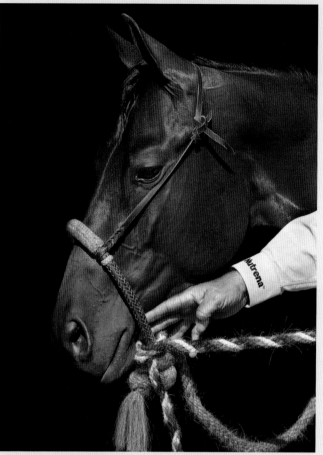

Correct hackamore fit is important to achieving the desired training results.

and should be used appropriately, and with an awareness that it can scare a horse in the hackamore if he's too green to handle any additional bite.

It also is a common mistake to use a stouter, harder hackamore than the one currently in use when a horse starts fighting his work; in many cases, doing just the opposite proves beneficial. Changing to a softer hackamore often allows a rider to work through a problem without instilling resentment and hurt, which can trigger an animal's flight-or-fight instinct, especially if a horse already has been skinned a little by the hackamore.

It's wise to have a thick, soft rope hackamore with a rawhide nose in your tack room. In instances when a horse's jaw line is tender, rather than take the horse out of the hackamore, you can switch to the hackamore with soft rope cheeks, raise or lower it a bit on the horse's head, and continue training. The last thing you want your horse to remember

is that the hackamore "bit" him—and then he was taken out of it. Changing to the soft hackamore allows training to continue while being mindful of the horse.

Consider the bone structure and flesh of each animal as you choose a hackamore. Soft- and thin-skinned individuals cannot tolerate the coarsely braided hackamore that a thick-hided horse can tolerate, and likely get along better in a smoother, higher-plait hackamore. It is also critical to monitor each horse's feel, how he responds, as well as the condition of his jaw and nose, and make changes in the hackamore setting, fit, or style to accommodate the horse.

The sequence of the various hackamores used on one horse during training might be very different from that used with another horse. The ability to adapt as a trainer is important. Know that each animal's training journey is like a unique braid, made from different strands in a pattern all its own.

The Fiador

The definition of the word "fiador" in its equestrian connotation is ambiguous, but is thought to be of South American origin. In the 18th century the word "fiador" was translated from Spanish into English as "surety" or "bond," and referenced a variety of purposes, including the long line used to train hawks in falconry. In all instances the word pertains to safekeeping of some sort. In relation to the hackamore, the fiador is the keeper and stabilizer of the headgear, guarding the hackamore to keep it from coming off the horse when he is being led or is tied.

In the old days, when rank 5-year-old broncs were blindfolded, saddled, unleashed and bucked-out for breaking, the fiador was used to keep the hackamore from flying off the horse's head during the clash. As soon as that mount settled into his work, the fiador was removed and then used only when the cowboy was afoot.

The hobbling action of the fiador on the heel knot prevents the hackamore from moving freely up the horse's jaw when the reins are engaged, and also from falling back to a neutral release-point at the chin. It is, therefore, uncommon to see a hackamore trainer schooling his mount with the fiador in place, even though he probably has one handy or can improvise one when he steps down from the saddle. Should an animal balk, spook, or pull back, a hackamore without a fiador likely can be pulled from underneath the horse's chin and come off his head.

A simple tie of the mecate rein around the throatlatch creates a makeshift fiador to ensure the animal's safekeeping. It is imperative to keep enough slack in the mecate that the heel knot isn't pulled back into the horse's jaw, causing him discomfort and confusion. Keep in mind that the hackamore is not to be tied back, but rather gently hobbled to prevent it from being pulled over the horse's chin.

Bring the mecate rein up the horse's neck to rest just behind the ears, keeping the slack out of the offside rein.

Then form a loop on the near side, using your left hand to grasp the rein under your horse's head, as shown, with the end of the loop rein in your right hand.

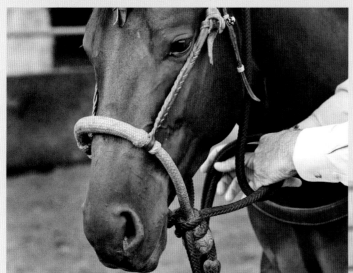

Bring the end of the loop rein end around both reins in your left hand, as shown.

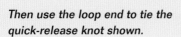

Then use the loop end to tie the quick-release knot shown.

Holding the Mecate

Anyone can put a hackamore on a horse, take up the mecate, and start training, just as he could braid rawhide in hopes of building a hackamore. An unschooled hand attempting either skill can fashion a similar product, but one lacking the foundation, uniformity, and the desirable traits that allow the article to function properly.

Rough, fumbling, or forceful cues to the horse are somewhat like strands of rawhide crossed out of sequence in a sloppy braid. A real hackamore horse is as complex a creation as a 40-plait braid and even more delicate and time-consuming to build. Handling a mecate with unrefined hands damages the feel and balance necessary in training, leaving a poorly turned-out horse to show for it. The very spirit of patience and diligence that forms the hackamore from rough strands into a serviceable work of art stands as a reminder to the trainer: There are no shortcuts or fast tracks to building a hackamore horse, only proper preparation, skilled work, consistency, and time.

Any tool used incorrectly can boondoggle a project, often to the point of being irreparable. The hackamore is no different. Proper grip of the mecate is gentle, with open fingers on the rein—never a death-grip. A dull grip produces a dull horse, and one who lays into the pressure of the heavy hand. The hackamore, by its artful design, is never to be pulled on mindlessly, but rather to be operated by an artistic mechanic.

Follow the sequence shown to encourage the lightness sought in a well-schooled hackamore horse.

The first signal to your horse comes when the fingers of your initially open hand close around the rein. Your horse feels that change and is alerted that something is about to happen.

Next, slide your hand down the mecate to give your horse further opportunity to think and respond.

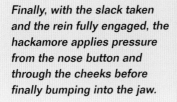

Finally, with the slack taken and the rein fully engaged, the hackamore applies pressure from the nose button and through the cheeks before finally bumping into the jaw.

When your horse gives by flexing laterally to follow the rein, you must promptly release your grip to give your horse a reward.

In time, good handling—in the form of a signal, command, consequence and reward—trains your horse to react to the minimal cue of your grip changing on the rein.

The rule of thumb is to keep your hands in an imaginary box, which is saddle-gullet width, belt-level, and saddle-horn height. Traditionally, the small loop, held in your left hand, is formed to take up the slack so that there is no messy "drape" between your hands. This allows you to keep your hands within the box, and also can leave your right hand free for roping, opening gates and such.

Softness in the hackamore horse is nurtured into being, not forced, and softness requires a rider to utilize good timing through his feel of the reins. Feel comes in the form of subtleties and is developed only by those who take the time to seek it. The gentle, open grip should not be forgotten as it allows for the greatest feel and softest handle on the horse.

Should you find yourself in the middle of a fight with your horse, the first thing to do is to stop pulling the rein. Don't get into a pulling contest with your horse, whatever you do. Instead, return to bumping and working the hackamore on the horse's nose and jaw. When you give a horse something to pull against, he pulls, and no matter how strong you are, he wins.

"The trainer who hurries doesn't cheat time—only himself and his horse."

5

Introducing Your Horse to the Hackamore

Whether the hackamore is used during a horse's first training session or his hundredth, and regardless of how well-broke he might be in the snaffle, the hackamore requires introduction to the horse. Pressure created by hackamore cues translates differently with the hackamore using off-side pressure for a function or response versus the snaffle bit's cues with direct-side cheek pressure. Even a horse going well in the snaffle bit and performing all maneuvers with relative ease must be educated to understand the hackamore's different sensations on his face.

Often a green hackamore horse looks to the right in response to a right rein, as he's confused by the hackamore's cheek pressure. Consistency and repetition help the horse to differentiate between the direct-cheek pull of the snaffle and the off-side push of the hackamore and to grasp the concept of leverage.

Checking-up a horse, also commonly known as bitting-up, is a good way to introduce a horse to the different sensations experienced with the hackamore. By allowing the animal time to think about

what's happening to him, he can be more accepting of the hackamore pressure applied and is less apt to fight or be resistant to the hackamore.

Check-Up Laterally

Follow the sequence of steps shown to check-up your horse laterally and introduce him to the hackamore. Remember: Lateral bend is first and foremost in training, while vertical flexion comes later. Trapping your horse vertically at the poll before he's supple from side to side is like putting the proverbial cart before the horse.

A horse that bobs his head while tied around to the side is developing a vice that should be addressed as soon as it arises. You can discourage this behavior by taking the lead rope of the mecate under your horse's forearm and up to the saddle horn. If he's tied to the right, for example, take the lead rope up the left side of the saddle, or vice versa. Doing so imitates a rider's hands controlling the horse's nose, setting clearly defined parameters for the horse to find. Secure your lead rope as a

Groundwork is an effective way to introduce a horse to the hackamore and help him understand the different sensations a hackamore creates.

Start teaching your horse lateral flexion by taking the mecate rein over the saddle, behind the cantle. Adjust one side of the rein shorter than the other to tie or check your horse's head around to one side.

Determine an appropriate length of rein, allowing only enough tension that your horse finds relief with his head at a 90-degree angle to the side. Initially, to avoid panic, some horses might require an even looser 45-degree tie-around in the first session. Watch your animal's expression; the eyes and ears display his level of comfort or discomfort so you can adjust the rein accordingly for the situation. Secure the mecate rein by hitching it with the saddle strings, taking care to ensure that the opposite-side rein has no contact with the hackamore.

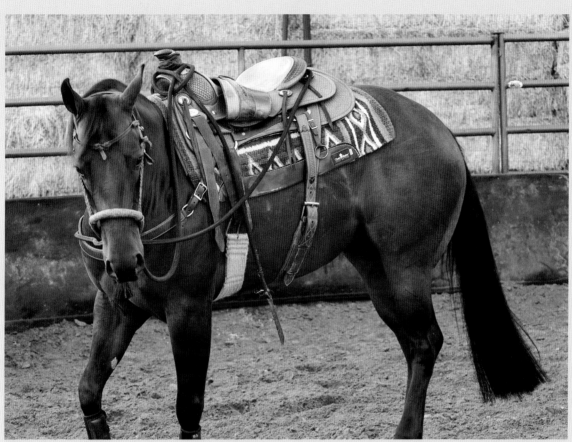

As you work, remember that you are not training only the face or poll of your animal, but are teaching him to give his body, spine, and feet as a whole to the pressure created by the hackamore. Encourage movement by clucking or calmly using a longe whip until your horse walks quietly in a small circle. It is crucial that the green horse learns to follow the pressure of the hackamore and seek relief by yielding. Allowing your horse to stand still and lay into the pressure numbs his facial nerves to the hackamore, teaching your horse a bad habit from the start. Similarly, overdoing the check-up by working your horse too long creates fatigue in his neck muscles and causes resentment.

Watch closely for small improvements. When your horse shows signs of softening and giving readily, it's time to untie him. Although some horses bend greatly, holding slack in the rein, others give in small, less dramatic increments, and both efforts must be rewarded. Trying to force a less limber, heavier horse to soften before he's learned to do so on his own leads only to a fight, causing upset, which slows the learning process further. You might wish to ask your horse for a lot, but be satisfied with a little.

boundary, not as a restraint, leaving enough slack that your horse merely bumps into pressure if he thrusts out his nose out or bobs his head up and down. The correct application is one with consequence, not restriction.

Be aware of any negative tendencies your horse displays when checking-up or any groundwork is performed. A keen trainer is ever watchful and recognizes the natural abilities, as well as the limitations, of each horse. Knowing on which side the animal is stiff or how much pressure he can handle are a few of the clues that help when designing an effective training program for each individual horse.

It is important to curtail any vices in this early stage of training and, therefore, wise to monitor your green horse closely. A bad habit learned during the groundwork stage can carry into riding and can multiply rapidly. If you don't want a given behavior when you're on your horse's back, don't let him do it when you work him on the ground.

Every phase of groundwork plays a vital role in your horse's progression. Never advance to a new exercise if the current exercise has not yet been mastered. Allow time for your training to "cure" and take full effect, so that your horse doesn't come apart farther down the road.

Longeing and Giving

After your horse is somewhat accustomed to the lateral bitting-up, or checking, he is ready to be taught to give to the hackamore while he moves on the longe line. Consider this phase of training to be like cutting strands of rawhide before you can braid. Although not as glamorous a job as later work, it is an important job and never should be hurried. This preparatory work sets the stage for everything to come, and when done correctly, makes building a hackamore horse a little easier than it otherwise might be.

To begin, slide a soft line under your horse's chin, through the V of the hackamore, and loop it around his neck at the poll.

Tie a bowline or other knot that can't tighten down and choke your horse, leaving a pleasant amount of slack at the throatlatch.

As you send your horse away at a walk or trot, gently work the hackamore on his nose by bumping the line, and watch for clues to the animal's comfort level. Often chewing and licking behavior ensues, signs that your horse is relaxing into the task he's been given.

The softening of your horse's jaw and tongue are good indicators that you can begin to ask for more movement by sending your horse into a lope. He should travel with his neck relaxed in a natural manner and have a calm, attentive expression.

67

After longeing your horse several revolutions around the pen, with your horse displaying signs of willingness, ask him to stop by saying "whoa" and give a check on the longe line. If your horse stiffens in response and raises his head, he needs to be softened to the hackamore by bumping the line until he gives his nose. Assuming he has been schooled appropriately in the lateral tie-around, he should seek relief in the stop fairly readily. Continue starting and stopping in the same direction until your horse gives to a bump on the hackamore and comes to a complete halt, free of resistance.

Remember that horses are bilateral creatures. When you begin working in the opposite direction, prepare to encounter some stiffness and resistance all over again. Your horse might even behave as if the exercise is completely new to him, simply because the opposite side of his body is now being worked. Repeat the same procedures with calm authority until he demonstrates forward motion and performs stops fluidly and with similar suppleness and respect in each direction.

Vertical Flexion on the Line

During groundwork, a good trainer shapes and refines a horse into a willing, pliable form, setting up the horse for an improved chance of success under saddle. With a little time and a few additional processes, your mount can be ready for the complex stages of his training.

As with a rawhide strand in the flesher, a horse's flaws and bad tendencies are removed by a process of elimination, one step at a time, until the desired workable state is achieved. Bitting- or checking-up your horse vertically is another step in the refining process the prospective hackamore horse must undergo, but should be introduced only after his lateral flexion and longeing responses are solid.

Follow these guidelines and remain ever attuned to your horse's eyes and ears as you proceed; his expressions foretell his actions. In the interests of safety and progress, you want to keep your animal in a settled, calm state, making whatever modifications necessary in the setup to ensure the best possible experience for your horse.

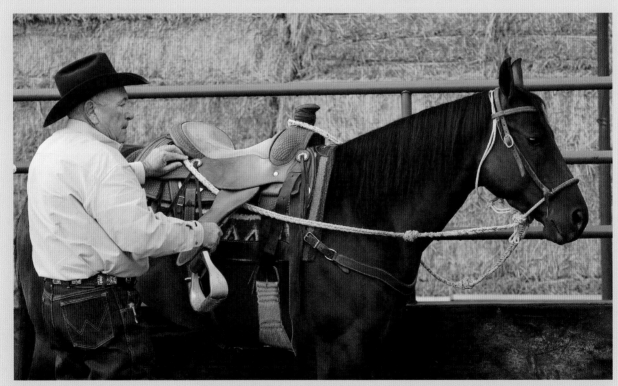

When using split reins, as shown, bring the right rein under the stirrup and around behind the cantle so you can tie it on the near side when working your horse to the left. When using a mecate, take your loop rein over the cantle of your saddle and then tighten the rein by pulling the slack through the mecate wraps, which extends your lead rope.

On the near side, tie the two reins together near the cantle. With split reins or a mecate, adjust either type of rein so that your horse finds relief from the hackamore by bringing his nose into a vertical position, and no further. Tying too tightly too early on can cause a horse to panic, leading to fear or an accident.

Send your horse out at a walk or trot, allowing him time to feel the hackamore and think through the exercise. Do not push him to lope before he's ready. Once he's calm and flexes at the poll, you can send him on to the lope and repeat the same stopping exercise discussed previously.

Some resistance and even reluctance to move forward at this stage are not uncommon and should be dealt with in a manner that diffuses upset in the horse, rather than igniting it. Make this a confidence-building experience by not overworking your horse. Then find a good spot to end the session when your horse moves freely and gives his head, even if only a little. In a matter of time and with quality sessions, your horse gradually can accept increased pressure and vertical flexion in the hackamore.

The Hard-Set

There comes a time during the training of every horse when he tests you. Most groundwork is choreographed to deal with these challenges particularly, so they do not arise when you're in the saddle. A runaway, for example, is one of the most dreaded things to any hackamore trainer, and a problem that is to be avoided and trained out of a horse at all cost.

Using the hard-set enables a runaway to be simulated and swiftly corrected, reinforcing to your horse that the hackamore is the ultimate authority. Performed correctly, this exercise convinces the animal that he can be stopped at any given moment, regardless of his speed.

Have patience, as your horse likely resists the set and jerks his head up the first few times you stop him. If your horse doesn't start giving to the set after a few repetitions, you

Your neck rope for longeing, previously mentioned, should be in place. Secure your mecate rein through the gullet and over your saddle horn, initially without rein contact on the hackamore. Let your horse move on the line for a few laps, and then encourage him to travel faster down the long side of your pen by walking quickly after him.

Your horse might bolt a bit, heading down the rail away from you with speed, and this should not be discouraged. Allowing him to try to leave you gives this exercise great impact. The hard-set is accomplished as your horse speeds away. You, as handler, must step back and abruptly take hold of the longe line, causing your horse to double-back over his hocks, yield to the hackamore and face you.

can tie the lead rope under his forearm and to the saddle horn, as described in the previous tying-around exercise. As with a lateral tie-around, do not tie the lead rope to hold down your horse's head, but to allow enough slack so that the lead catches the hackamore only when your horse throws his nose out of position.

This hard-set exercise instills in your horse a belief in the hackamore's supremacy. The exercise teaches your horse to give by bending his entire body, driving an inside hind foot deeply underneath his body for balance. After a few such sets, your horse sees that it's much easier to avoid making that contact by being attentive and yielding the instant he feels slack taken from the line. This cements in his mind that there is no method to outrun the hackamore and helps to extinguish future problems. In the event that your horse does try to take you for a ride at some point in his training, when he has been hard-set from the ground, he remembers and respects the bite of the hackamore more than a horse that hasn't experienced a hard-set.

Ground-Driving

From checking-up, longeing, and setting, your horse has become well-acquainted with the hackamore and now should be giving humbly to pressure on his nose and jaw. Before you step aboard, however, test how well you've prepared your horse for riding by driving him. If you've completed the groundwork thoroughly, culling vices and alleviating stiffness along the way, this exercise flows smoothly, proving that your horse is ready to ride.

The best way to simulate riding while you remain on the ground, driving your horse allows you to bump and rock the hackamore in much the same way you do when you take the reins from atop your horse's back. While using the driving lines, should you encounter resistance as you maneuver your animal through turns and stops, it's time to put a little more thought into where things have gone wrong, and then take the necessary measures to fix any problems and eliminate resistance. You might have to go back to the bitting-up and hard-setting exercises in

To ground-drive your horse in the hackamore, you need four rings large enough for the longe lines to pass through the rings easily, as well as four pieces of string or latigo. Attach a ring to each cheek of the hackamore, just above the mecate wraps, and fasten the remaining two rings to each back-cinch rigging.

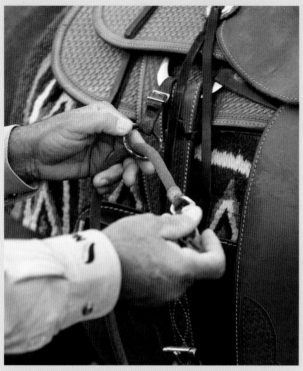

After the driving lines have been passed through the saddle rings, snap them into the rings on the hackamore.

The rings on the saddle allow the driving lines to slide and not hang up, which is of utmost importance for the hackamore to function properly. Sometimes driving lines are run through the stirrups, but setting the rings and lines high on the horse more accurately resembles how the reins work when you're riding.

Move your horse forward and think about rocking the hackamore on his nose, just as you do when riding— giving when he gives, bumping when he doesn't. If your horse holds his face in a vertical position respectful of the hackamore, reward him by allowing a fair amount of slack in the lines. When your horse's head comes out of the vertical position, again bump one line or the other intermittently to soften his response.

Once your horse moves and drives willingly with proper carriage, stop him by saying whoa, setting your inside line while bumping the outside line. You can back your horse in the same fashion, being aware to hold one line and work the other, never pulling solidly on both lines at the same time.

combination with ground-driving for a time. These exercises further instill the fundamentals your horse must have before you mount him to ride.

When driving your horse, reverse him by relinquishing your hold on the inside line as you take all slack from the line outside, increasing your bumps on the hackamore until your horse turns through the reverse. You then can help drive him forward in the new direction by slapping the line he's moving away from against his side, to mimic your leg when riding.

Ground-drive your horse in each direction, stopping, turning and backing until he follows his nose laterally and gives vertically the way you would like when he's being ridden. Do not expect perfection the first day your horse is in the driving lines, though there should be no signs of rudeness or opposition either. A horse tells you when he's ready to ride, so be mindful and appreciative of your horse's small advances and build on those from day to day.

The trainer who hurries doesn't cheat time—only himself and his horse. The era of the vaqueros is called "the land of *mañana*" for this very reason. "Mañana" means tomorrow or an unspecified future time, and that word that should be part of the anthem for

> **"'Mañana' means tomorrow... and that word that should be part of the anthem for every training program. Good training takes patience— there always is tomorrow."**

every training program. Good training takes patience—there always is tomorrow.

73

"It looked to me like that man came to Earth on horseback; looked odd to see him walkin'."
—Ernie Morris, regarding Rod Howard, La Panza Ranch

6

Key Points Under Saddle

There is much to be learned by watching. Standing alongside an arena fence, observing riders school their mounts, often can teach one something about himself. Some riders appear hurried, others vexed, some oblivious. Most stare at their horses' heads and do not see; the riders give commands but never listen. Rare are the true horsemen, tuned-in heart and soul to the horses beneath them.

If you have an opportunity to observe the smooth orchestration of a real horseman at work, it might just open your eyes to the world of subtleties and silent communications that connect him to his mount. The horse doesn't speak with words, but the horseman hears everything his mount has to say. The horseman trains with all his senses, always one step ahead of the animal, in a seamless conversation. No order is given mindlessly, no action wasted. Very matter-of-factly, the horseman stacks the cards in his favor, artfully compelling the animal to yield his power and do his rider's bidding.

The vaqueros of old California lived in harmony with their horses, right down to the details of their equipment. The dangling spur chains under the heels of the vaquero's boots, for example, often are thought to have been ornamental. But make no mistake; although the Californio was a fancy dresser, each and every part of his ensemble had significance. Those spur chains, accompanied by the slobber chains on the reins, jangled as he rode, encouraging his mount to find a good cadence and effectively cover ground.

If modern riders consider their horses with the same tenacity, they must acknowledge the importance of every cue and every detail in each piece of tack, from their headstalls right down to their spurs. Surely then riders today would become better listeners and, in turn, better trainers than they are.

The horse is not an accessory, nor a servant, but an asset, with athletic mastery infinitely beyond that of most humans. His fierce yet willing spirit calls to his rider's very heart. Thus, the horse is teacher to a willing student. Every good horseman studies his horses, memorizes and learns their habits until he knows those horses better than they know themselves.

"Slow-riding" a horse builds his confidence and gives him time to master the basic skills that are the foundation for advanced maneuvers.

Prepare to Ride

It is wise to incorporate the new with the familiar in any stage of horse training. When you're ready to ride your hackamore horse for the first time, begin the session with the groundwork to which he's grown accustomed. By working him on the longe or driving him, you allow your horse to get into his comfort zone with a workmanlike outlook and a relaxed mind. After a few laps, he can be ready for you to step aboard. Your horse has been refreshed to the feeling of the hackamore on his nose and is set up for a successful, confidence-building first ride.

If you've never before ridden with a mecate, you're probably wondering what to do with the lead once you're in the saddle. Here are a few options for fastening the lead when you're horseback.

There are a couple different ways to tie the mecate lead to the saddle when riding. You can simply hitch the lead to the horn. Start by wrapping the mecate lead around the horn.

Now pull the lower strand of the mecate lead on the horn up and out to make a loop, as shown, pinching the loop closed with your thumb.

Next, rotate the loop, bringing the left side of the loop over toward the near side of the saddle horn.

"If you've never before ridden with a mecate, you're probably wondering what to do with the lead once you're in the saddle."

Drop the second rotated loop over the saddle horn to complete the hitch. Don't forget to pull the hitch snugly around your horn.

Or you can coil the lead into neat loops to be tied to your saddle. Always measure the proper length before you secure the lead to the saddle, ensuring a happy medium of sufficient slack in the lead without excess draping. Flip the coiled lead around so that the tail of the lead faces forward, where it is less likely to feed out slack as you ride.

Use your saddle strings to secure the mecate lead. Take the latigo over and around the coils.

Then make a loop and a half hitch on top, so that you form a quick-release knot, and then pull the knot snug.

Now bring the lower saddle string up to rotate it and make a loop much like you do when hitching your lead over your horn.

Drop the lower string loop over the first loop you made. Then snug the second loop around the first loop.

That also forms a quick-release knot, making it easy to untie your lead. When the strings are tied correctly, a pull on that open-loop latigo tail causes your lead to come loose and fall away. Should a cow collide with your horse and become entangled, you can free yourself and avert potential disaster.

Lateral Flexion

Begin riding your horse with a simple task in mind. Riding a small circle is a good place to start. This small circle has been simulated in the previous bitting-up process when the hackamore rein was checked to one side. If you've done your homework, your horse should be adequately prepared and willing to follow the rein when you are in the saddle.

Using the soft, open fingers previously described, start moving your horse forward at a walk. Follow the sequence of closing your grip, sliding your hand down the rein, and finally engaging the hackamore to communicate the desired lateral flexion to your horse and shape him on the circle.

When your horse gives his nose and seeks a relief point by yielding, reward him by opening your fingers. Give back to your horse only the slack that he does not take from you. In other words, if you soften the rein and he begins to take that slack by pulling in the other direction, take him around again in a circle to show him that he must maintain his carriage, his frame. When he can hold a lateral bend on a soft rein, without taking away the slack you give, your horse truly is carrying himself in the proper frame.

This simple procedure needs to be solid at the walk before progressing to the jog, and then consistently solid at the jog before you ever lope. You might be tempted to

The checking-up groundwork exercise described in the previous chapter prepares your horse to follow your rein when you ride and ask him to stay in frame.

Your horse must learn how to use his hindquarters to maintain proper carriage at a walk before he's able to hold his frame at the trot or lope.

rush ahead, but remember that if your horse learns he can escape you in the hackamore, he never "unlearns" that.

Take the time to lay a solid foundation by "slow-riding" your horse. Slow-riding means just that—slow, confidence-building training that allows your horse to develop the skill set he needs for every other upcoming maneuver. Pushing ahead to turns, stops, and faster speeds without this sound base in place can be the undoing of your hackamore horse.

Each animal progresses at a different rate, with some settling in to the slow-riding with softness and appropriate carriage and form in a matter of a few rides. Other horses continue to try to take the slack from the rein when you soften your hands, and such horses need more miles of the basics before advancing in their training.

Punishing a horse for not absorbing these concepts by riding him hard or jerking him around only sets him further behind, potentially ruining him to the hackamore. Intimidation cannot replace true, sound training. A horse that gives to his rider from fear is not yielding to his rider's hands, but merely hiding—and he can hide for only so long before trying to escape.

Vertical Flexion

Once your horse follows your grip-and-slide lateral rein cue and moves willingly at all three gaits, you can introduce vertical flexion by way of the rocking or bumping motion previously presented in the ground-driving material. At the walk, rock your hands, one hand and then the other, in a motion complimentary to the walk's four-beat stride,

When teaching vertical flexion, the rocking or bumping motion of your hands is compatible with the rhythm of your horse's gait.

moving the hackamore on the horse's nose until he wants to get away from the bumping by flexing at the poll and tucking in his nose.

Use your legs to drive your horse up and into the hackamore. If you're accustomed to applying strong leg cues when your horse is in a snaffle, you might find that a more delicate leg aid is required. You want to encourage your horse to ride up into the hackamore, yet not go through it.

Handling the hackamore requires rhythm and timing that mirrors the movement, speed, and action unique to each horse at each gait. At the jog, both hands bump in harmony with the two-beat stride. Remember that you want your horse to seek the center of the hackamore and to yield his nose to the motion.

When loping, your hands take on a rolling action, with your inside rein a little high and with you bumping that rein a little more than the outside rein to elevate your horse's leading shoulder. Just as with the walk and jog, utilize a rhythm compatible with the gait, a three-beat lope. Your horse should give his face to the hackamore, tucking his nose in an effort to keep the hackamore cheeks from

The goal is to teach your horse to flex at the poll with his nose on the vertical, rather than drop his neck and head from the withers.

contacting his jawbone. In this position, he should feel absolutely light, never hanging heavily on your hands.

The Headset

An element of grave importance is your horse's headset in the hackamore. Do not misconstrue a dropping-off of his neck and head for collection. Your horse must flex at the poll with his nose vertical, creating a slight arc through the neck, with his weight rocked back and over his hocks. In this position, the entire spine is engaged and your horse's front end is light.

If you teach your hackamore horse to drop at the withers, packing his head too low, he learns to push straight down through the hackamore and evade your direction. It is much harder to revoke a bad habit than it is to avoid one in the first place. Although conformation plays a significant role in the frame your horse can carry, remember that riding your horse up and into the hackamore equates to lightness. A flat-necked, nose-to-the-floor headset is not only undesirable, but also unproductive.

Sometimes a naturally low-headed horse might need encouragement to float atop the hackamore and attain the best possible carriage. Help such a horse to grasp the desired frame by elevating your hands and bumping skyward as you drive with enough leg to create energy and lift. When your horse responds by gathering himself and coming up and into the hackamore, relax your cues. Repeat these steps when your horse tries to

flatten out, keeping your instructions concise and consistent. Through patience and repetition, your horse can find a position of carriage that corresponds to his natural, low neck-set, yet keeps his shoulders and front feet light.

Connect His Face to His Feet

Horses often are nagged, checked, and yanked by riders who, somewhere in the fray, have forgotten about their horses from the poll back. The simple fact is that head carriage is merely the result of a properly or improperly aligned horse. All the contraptions and training in the world can't put an attractive, natural-looking headset in front of a heavy, misaligned body.

As you ride and train, remember that you are riding your horse, not his face. Your job is to guide his footfall by aligning his body from his tail to his nose in a shape suited for a specific task. Teaching your horse proper balance from the hindquarters enables him

From a standstill, maintain contact with your right rein while making small bumps on the left rein to encourage your horse to back. Soften your contact and bumping as a reward when he complies and steps backward.

Once your horse backs calmly and freely, cease bumping the left rein altogether, and increase your contact on the right rein. By making small bumps with contact on that rein, you encourage your horse to bend laterally to the right.

"...keep in mind that your horse's nose must relate to his hind feet."

Due to the backward motion, your horse naturally curves his spine as he gives in response to your direction, sitting down to balance over his hindquarters. Since he already has been taught to follow his nose, your contact and bumping leads him through a half-turn over his right hock, thereby making the connection of the right rein to his right hind.

to perform with a high degree of athleticism. With his rear-end drive in use, his movements are dramatic, swift, and fluid, and his spine is engaged. This results in floating natural carriage and a consistent headset, not to mention a happier horse.

In all the maneuvers that you perform, keep in mind that your horse's nose must relate to his hind feet. This is the basic principle of collection and the core of hackamore training. As with the rawhide artisan building a hackamore, you've gone through preparatory phases to shape your horse into fine, workable parts; you've removed the faults, cured, and tempered him. But all this work and preparation is in vain without a properly built core upon which to base all other, more elaborate training.

Having a solid core means that, in response to a drawn rein, your horse surrenders his nose, rounds his spine, and drives his hind end

deeply beneath his body. It is due only to this true collection that properly performed stops, spins, rollbacks, and all other skills demonstrated by a fine riding horse are possible.

Help your horse to connect his face to his feet by consciously riding his body and directing his feet through the hackamore. Backing your horse into a turn is a great way to teach the face-to-foot connection and create a solid basis for future training.

Follow these easy steps below to begin establishing that all-important core, the face-to-foot connection around which you can build your hackamore horse.

When you've made that 180-degree turn, casually walk your horse in the other direction. Work both sides of your horse in the same manner until he moves evenly and willingly as he backs into a turn in either direction.

A common problem is a horse not maintaining a proper frame. Instead of being light on the forehand because he's driving from his back end, the horse instead seems heavy on the forehand and strung out in the rear. Initially, to elevate his forehand, bump upward lightly on the reins to try and remedy the situation.

If your light bumps don't encourage your horse to reshape his frame and work off his back end, become a bit more assertive. But remember that you also must drive your horse forward into that desirable, collected frame.

You find that in a matter of a few backing-turns, your horse associates the rein directly to his hind pivot foot and drives it under his belly to roll into the new direction. In time, this simple exercise is used to develop the rollback, spin, sliding stop, and other maneuvers requiring advanced collection.

The Big Release

Between maneuvers, when standing quietly, you can continue to show your horse that there is reward in giving to the hackamore. Often when his feet are still, his brain has time to relax and simmer down, allowing him to better absorb and process information. In some cases, when a horse's stress or confusion level has risen, you can avert a fight and accomplish more by taking a time-out, bringing his flight-instinct-laced feet to a standstill. Doing some very elementary work with a big reward not only brings your horse's focus and willingness back on track, but also carries into other exercises when he again moves and his brain becomes a little busier.

The big release is a simple exercise, more for the horse's mind than his body, which further instills the laws of cause and effect. Take the reins and bump back and forth, left-right-left-right, perhaps with a little more exaggeration than you normally use when riding. Make your motions obvious, but not intimidating to your horse. When he surrenders his nose and arches his neck and flexes willingly, reward him immediately with a big release of slack in the reins.

Your horse might pull his head and nose right back out of frame. If he does, simply repeat the previous steps. You make the statement that great reward awaits, but only when your horse is in that one position.

When a horse understands how to respond softly and drive forward into the hackamore without going through it, he can regain the proper frame to travel smoothly. In other words, his face and his feet have reconnected.

To teach your horse that a big-release reward awaits him, bump first one rein and then the other a bit more obviously than usual.

When your horse gives his nose and flexes willingly, give him an equally obvious big release of the reins.

As opposed to making the animal feel trapped, which causes frustration and a fight, the big release concept sets boundaries for your horse, which he can choose to uphold or to disobey. The consequence for your horse not conceding and flexing his poll is made obvious by the more profound bumping action that you, the rider, display. Equally obvious, the release of the rein is dramatic to overemphasize the relief your horse finds when he's in compliance.

Rather than get into a fight and risk your horse running through the hackamore, you can use this simple release technique to turn off his engine, quiet his mind, and show him why he has reason to do things your way. What he learns through this simplistic form of fairness, consistency, and repetition mortars the foundation of all other performance to come.

Similarly, if you allow yourself to get caught in a moment of frustration and engage in a battle with your horse, rather than bring things down to a controllable level, that frustration also carries into all other areas of training. You cannot force your horse into the hackamore; you must convince him that it's the only place to be.

Set the Stage

The purpose of the hackamore is to properly prepare your horse for the bridle, a fact that shouldn't be forgotten along the way. Although not every horse can be a great hackamore horse, or even a good one, what your animal learns from his time in the hackamore is priceless to his outcome as a finished horse. As you build your horse's athleticism around appropriate carriage of his body, keep in mind that all training must relate to one-handed riding in the end.

Once your horse willingly follows the hackamore, with his face connected to his feet in all aspects of slow-riding, you can start to incorporate the building blocks for neck-reining. Although your first inclination is to focus on what you want in your horse, you also must be mindful of what you don't want. When you envision a good bridle horse, see one that stays between the reins, guiding to the left off a right neck-rein; the soft giving of his nose to the left flows seamlessly through his aligned body. That horse is free of resistance and a graceful depiction of training time well-spent.

Now picture the less-than-ideal horses you've seen in the bridle. They cock their heads in a counter-arc toward the neck-rein, mouths open, stiff through their spines. In no way are these horses' faces connected to their feet, nor are they able to use their bodies properly for any movement. Somewhere in the course of training, these stiff, open-mouthed horses have been hauled off a neck-rein rather than taught to respect guidance by staying between both reins.

Introduce the Neck-Rein

To teach your horse to move off a neck-rein while keeping proper form is a mindful process. It requires that you, as the rider, be self-policing and ever vigilant. A common mistake when introducing neck-reining occurs when a rider pulls the rein across the horse's neck, which creates drag on the hackamore, thereby tipping the horse's nose in the wrong direction. Avoid such a transgression by changing your thinking. Do not neck-rein your horse by shoving him away from the outside rein, but by giving him an opening into which he can move.

Introduce the new neck-rein command on familiar ground when your animal is quiet and calm. The backing-turn previously used to connect his face to his hind feet is a great place to start. Since your horse already is accustomed to the movement and his body can take the ideal form, adding the neck-rein here begins a good habit from day one.

Perform the backing-turn as before, but this time, as you increase the pull and bumping on the turn-rein, or direct rein, apply the outside rein in a rubbing motion against your horse's neck. Take care to have no contact on the hackamore with the outside, rubbing rein; your horse should feel only the mecate against his hide. The rubbing neck-rein tells your horse to move away while the direct rein tells him where to go and how to get there.

Being a creature of habit, your horse with repetition can move his form to function smoothly, eventually moving off the neck-rein to stay between both reins while carrying his body in the ideal form with the face-to-foot connection. This time-consuming process is not learned in a matter of weeks or months, but is instilled in your horse throughout his entire journey in the hackamore.

When introducing the neck-rein, the outside rein should only rub against the horse's neck without making any real contact with the hackamore.

7

Build Your Hackamore Horse's Skills

By now, you have introduced your horse to the hackamore, and he's learned about both lateral and vertical flexion, as well as the basics of neck-reining. He's familiar with the big release that provides a well-earned reward and moment of rest for his efforts. Equally important, your horse grasps the connection between his face and his feet, how a change in the hackamore rein directly affects his carriage and movement, a core basic for him to progress to advanced maneuvers.

In this chapter you build on the basic skills already established to advance your horse to the next level of performance. With the circling exercises and other drills presented here, your horse becomes supple and responsive as he masters the turnaround, the rundown and the stop.

Athletic Circles

This circling exercise can be built only on the face-to-foot core connection established earlier and focuses your hackamore horse's energy into further developing his athleticism. The goal and purpose of the athletic-circle drill is to introduce dynamic

movement while your horse's body is within the ideal frame. Here's how to develop such athletic movement while circling your horse.

Work in both directions until your horse can double back athletically and with confidence between the circles. Have enough patience between rollbacks to calmly jog multiple circles so there is no anticipation of the rollback when your horse nears the wall. Should your horse try to do a rollback on his own, calmly stop the motion and bring him back to the original circle. You might have to jog many times around the circle before again rolling him back in the other direction. Even if that means doubling your horse far fewer times than you had in mind, it is imperative to teach him to wait for your guidance so he does not learn to outthink you.

Once your horse performs the drill solidly in close proximity to the fence, move to circle him in the open. Without the use of the wall for a brake, the exercise must be modified slightly; in this case, you simply quit riding just prior to asking your horse for the turn.

To quit riding, relax in your saddle and sit in the stop position that you would assume when saying

The more solid your horse's foundation skills, the more easily he can achieve an advanced meneuver and, for example, "pedal" his way to a soft stop.

With your horse at a jog, ride a 15-foot circle close to the arena wall or fence. Let your horse settle into the circle until an even cadence and symmetry in your circle has been established. If you are in correct form on the circle, ideally your horse should come into the fence at a 45-degree angle, travel alongside it for only one stride, and then again make a 45-degree angle as he moves away from the fence. Allowing your horse to flatten-out and follow the arena wall or fence line degrades the shape of your circle and compromises this drill in its entirety.

A properly balanced horse can work in a circle again and again and in the same tracks without traveling off the arc of the circle or diving to the inside of it. When your horse consistently jogs a circle to the right, for example, and you near the 45-degree position, reach down your left, wall-side rein to make contact with the hackamore, and direct your horse's nose into the wall. In this 45-degree setup, your horse is inclined to roll over his hocks to follow the rein, his hind legs driving well underneath him for balance and impulsion.

Use small bumps on the direct rein keep your horse's nose soft through the turn and on course as he again sets out on a well-shaped circle, but now traveling in the other direction, to the left. If this maneuver is executed accurately, your horse comes out of the rollback to follow the same tracks of the previous circle and without any deviation.

When your horse circles and turns back comfortably on the fence, it's time to perform the same maneuver in the open. You can always go back to the fence, if necessary, to reinforce the desired response.

"whoa." However, in this exercise no verbal command is given. As your horse gathers himself in response to your body position, take the rein as before and double him back over his hocks to go in the new direction. Again, be careful to come out of the turn and travel in the previous circle's tracks.

Since the wall is not there to help you complete the turn, make sure to use enough leg pressure so that your horse turns over his hind foot with his entire body in ideal form as it comes through the maneuver. When you double back to the right, your left leg should create a barrier blocking your horse's ribcage and hip, to keep them from swinging to the left as you make the right turn. When you double to the left, use your right leg to keep your horse's body in alignment.

Should you experience a little trouble with this circle drill while riding away from the fence, fall back on the foundation work your horse already can perform well. Trying to power through the problem with brute force can be a regrettable and potentially devastating mistake. Instead, re-establish the core principle of the face-to-foot connection by stopping and backing a step or two before doubling your horse. By doing so, you can realign your horse's body to balance his carriage between his nose and pivot foot.

Especially when a horse is in the hackamore, it always is wise to slow down things when a problem arises; reassert your authority and nullify any challenge. By reverting to a drill that allows you to regain control, you prove to your horse that he cannot cheat or get away from the hackamore.

In-and-Out Circle Exercise

When your horse can perform the athletic circles consistently, rolling left to right and back left again, it's time to work the same-side-to-same-side, in-and-out circle drill. As before, jog your horse in a 15-foot circle and soften your body into the stop position. But this time, you turn your horse to the inside of the circle. When you travel to the right, for example, you halt and roll your horse back to the right, either beginning a new circle adjacent the one you previously were riding, or moving the horse through a full turn before returning to the original circle at a trot.

With the same control as before, you now should be able to make symmetrical circles in the ground and without wandering about the arena. When you've made several good

Travel to the left, for example, on a small circle with your horse traveling in frame. Then relax in your saddle before making contact with the left rein and bumping it.

As your horse halts, his nose in the hackamore softly follows your rein. He then rolls over his left hind foot to start the turn, which can be a 180-degree or a 360-degree turn, as shown.

When you work half-turns, your tracks in the ground illustrate a tidy figure eight, without the tracks wandering off the circles. In the full-turn variation, this exercise should leave a clean, correct circular track behind.

After the turn, send your horse out in another circle and make a few good passes around it. Then, as before, sit relaxed and again make contact with one rein to roll your horse back through himself and onto another circle.

passes from a right circle to a right turn, roll your horse in the opposite direction and work a left circle to a left turn. You need to complete several full circles between rollbacks or turns, keeping your horse's mind and body soft and responsive.

This goes without saying: When performing this drill and all others, you must not get so caught up in the moment or one movement that you forget the big picture. Hauling your horse through the drill, just to satisfy a turn, while sacrificing proper handling of the hackamore, is a catastrophic blunder. This circle-to-circle exercise shapes up well with relative ease for anyone who has done his homework properly and continues to utilize good hands on the mecate.

Remember the near-weightless feel of the handkerchief on the tabletop—a metaphor for the desired feel when you ride? Show your horse how to be light in hand by never giving him anything to pull against. Use these drills as roadways to lightness, not as attempts to circle and turn faster than you did before. When your horse learns to move his feet without any resistance in his body, all his movements gain agility, and his quickness develops with that agility.

Teach the Turnaround

From the circle-turn exercises, it is an easy transition to teach your horse the spin. At this point, your horse has learned to follow his nose, driving from his hindquarters while crossing over his front legs without interference in the turn. Because of this solid foundation, your horse now only needs to develop his carriage and hold his frame during consecutive revolutions in order to spin with proficiency.

The corner drill helps to guide your horse through a complete 360-degree turn, based on his aptitude for rolling back into the fence. Since he already is comfortable with turning toward the fence or wall, your horse should take to this new concept pretty quickly.

As in the previous exercise, you jog a 15-foot circle, only this time the circle is placed in the corner of the arena. When your horse is in the corner pocket between both fences, you sit down, soften your body, and move him into an inside turn, as you did in the previous drill. Your horse turns away from the wall to the inside of the circle. Once he completes the half-turn and with the arena fence now opposing you, it might seem that your horse has no place to go. However, your horse's familiarity with rolling through a turn and into the fence allows you to encourage him to drive on, sweeping through the rest of the turn for a full 360-degree revolution.

As your horse becomes confident, moving through the turnaround with softness and ease, you can ask for a second and third revolution. Do not rush into asking for six, seven or eight spins, however. Be happy with one

Ride your horse at a jog in a left-hand circle. As your horse enters the corner of the arena, prepare to turn left by bumping on the left rein.

Center your horse in the corner, between the two walls or fences, when you turn left to complete a 180-degree turn. Although it now seems the fence might block his efforts to complete a full revolution, remember that your horse already has learned how to roll into a fence.

Do not allow your horse's motion to cease, but urge him to continue turning to create a full 360-degree revolution, which places him back on the same trotting circle.

After your horse has developed his balance and cadence when turning in the corner, he's ready to work in the open.

and there. He soon learns that giving his all earns rest faster than making poor efforts repeatedly.

Also remember that each horse has an inborn level of talent to utilize, with some having light feet governed by fast-twitch muscles while other horses are lumbering and awkward. Work within the ability level of each animal you ride without asking him to be something that he cannot be.

It takes a special horse to end up with an awesome "40-plait-style" spin, and those who do have buzz-saw turns are born with that ability for their trainers to unleash. Most horses are far less fancy, some even as unrefined as a rugged eight-plait braid, and need to be taught how to spin with great patience. It is key to be realistic and fair with training goals, as these less talented horses can unravel when pressured to move in ways that are physically impossible for them. Instead, aim to lighten a heavy "eight-plait" spinner into a functional, working "12-plait" tool, and, just maybe, with the extra patience and time, he might surprise you by being a little better than expected in the end.

Sliding Stops

A beautifully trained horse performing a 30-foot sliding stop on a loose rein, his front feet pedaling freely, is a surefire head-turner. It's amazing that the horse, galloping down the arena, stops at all, let alone folds up like a willing accordion and sends up a blazing wave of sand as he cuts through the ground.

It is a safe bet to say that many folk, after seeing such a sight, have gone home and pulled a long-toothed roan out of the paddock, hell-bent to get a stop like that. Somewhere a poor old mare ends up with a rider aboard, kicking and spurring. Head up and eyes wide, the mare races down the arena, wondering if her rider has lost his mind. Just as she starts to get really worried, the rider slams down hard on the bridle, yelling, "WHOA!" at the top of his lungs. She throws her head straight up as the stainless steel bit floats her teeth, and bounces to a stop on braced front feet. This is the point when the rider looks back, scratches his head, rubs jolted vertebrae, and wonders what went wrong. Everything.

The soft-faced, rounded-spine, tail-in-the-dirt stop everyone desires is the grandest display of ultimate collection—the very manifestation of the face-to-feet-to-spine

or two spins performed well, with your horse maintaining a willing, unspoiled attitude, and build from there.

When your horse can spin pleasantly with balance and cadence in the corner, you can move the exercise a distance from the wall to work in the open. Be compassionate in teaching the turnaround, as it requires coordination, strength, and stamina unlike any other skill. You can sour a horse to spinning by fatiguing him, so it is of great importance not to overwork your horse. Aside from mentally ruining him to the turnaround, if he's worked to a point of muscular exhaustion, the risk of injury also increases.

For your horse to be his best, he must like what he's doing and find his efforts rewarded. If he turns a few times with fast, light feet and good form in the hackamore, quit him then

To perform like this, a physically fit athlete must be able to mentally make the face-to-foot connection.

connection and cultivated athleticism. Teaching your horse to stop properly begins the very first session, the first time he's subjected to rein contact. Teach him to follow his nose, to give and to find his reward, and you are setting him up to be a solid stopper. Likewise, if you haul on your horse's face, teaching him to throw up his nose in evasion, you can bet your truck and trailer he stops similarly to the old mare.

The core of your hackamore horse should be ready for building a stop, having been solidified by your slow-riding, circle-turn drills, and the other exercises previously outlined. The fundamentals of that core already have initiated the instinct for your horse to stop on his hocks, and as long as he continues to carry himself well with his body softly in frame, he's ready for advancement.

The One-Rein Stop

The one-rein stop replaces the usual ask-your-horse-for-a-maneuver, let-him-try-it, then-fix-what-he-did-wrong regimen by showing your horse how to respond to the stop command. Rather than allowing your horse to make an error and correcting him, you can condition him in a progressive manner to react to the word "whoa." The following drill accomplishes just that, setting the stage for the siding stop by conditioning your animal to respond as you desire.

To begin, lope a circle, being attentive to your horse's frame as he works in the hackamore. He should float, his carriage balanced and between the reins, never leaning in the direction of travel and never heavy in hand. His inside shoulder should be light and

The one-rein stop helps develop your horse's response to the word "whoa."

It's important in a one-rein stop to sit relaxed in your saddle and then say "whoa" before you ever take hold of the rein.

You also can use an arena wall or fence when working on "whoa" and the one-rein stop.

Timing is important. Don't forget to say "whoa" first, then make contact with the rein.

slightly elevated, creating more drive from his inside hock.

You can encourage this drive and elevation by offsetting your hands, lifting the inside rein while extending the outside rein lower and away. A bumping, rocking motion with your hands can help your horse find the center of the hackamore. In order to stay between your reins, he must lift his inside shoulder and drive the haunch farther beneath himself.

The one-rein stop is performed by simply sitting and saying whoa while taking contact on your outside rein to draw your horse over his hocks. Your horse has been taught to double, so his inclination is to follow his nose, thus driving from a pivot foot as he lightens his front end for the turn.

Soften your horse once or twice to be sure he's responsive and between the reins; then lope on the circle as you've done before. Be aware that you must give your commands in proper sequence—sit and speak, then take hold of the rein. If you grab that rein without giving the stop command first, you aren't teaching your horse that whoa means for him to get on his hocks; you're simply doubling him on the circle. After a few repetitions of sitting relaxed and speaking to your horse, he starts to drive his outside hind leg well under his belly in response to whoa, and the rein contact is soft.

Now take another lope around the circle, but this time, as you ask your horse to stop, follow your outside rein contact with a draw and a bump on the inside rein. Your horse already is driving his outside hind beneath him, and the unexpected inside rein contact causes him to respond by driving his other hock forward, so he sits down on both legs for a stop. Once stopped, you can back your horse softly to reinforce the stop-means-get-back concept, but do so reassuringly and finish with a reward of rest for your horse.

"The stop is only as good as the rundown leading to it."

This drill is a simple way to teach your horse the mechanics of the sliding stop and, if executed appropriately on a horse with any aptitude, yields results relatively quickly. Remember, you aren't looking for a lengthy slide early on, but a nice sitting-down action over your horse's hocks. As your horse becomes confident with the maneuver, you can gradually increase your speed, which adds length to the slide.

Should you encounter any problems with the one-rein stop in the open, take your horse to the perimeter of the arena, traveling alongside the wall, and rework the exercise. Using the wall helps to guide your horse over his hocks, thus giving him confidence in the drill.

Fence Your Horse

Now that your horse has learned to stop on the circle and can use both hocks in a balanced fashion with his nose soft in the hackamore, you can introduce stopping on a straight line. Fencing is a great way to teach your horse to lope a straight line from one end of the arena to the other and without deviation or anticipation.

Too often, a rider gets so caught up in thinking about the stop that he forgets about the approach to the stop, and one does not exist without the other. The stop is only as good as the rundown leading to it. An ideal rundown has speed, which is controlled by the rider, and his horse travels in good form, carrying himself well between the reins. The horse never increases speed of his own accord to charge through his rider's hands, but must willingly be guided from his first stride to the final one.

To fence your horse, first walk him down the straightaway path that you intend to lope, as this helps to show your horse what is going to be asked of him. Stay away from the arena side fences or walls, focusing instead on a specific target on the end wall in front of you. Keep your horse flexed softly between your reins; he should be straight from nose to tail, with no arc or crookedness in his body as he travels. When you arrive at the far end of the arena, quit riding and let your horse stand quietly with his nose close to the wall or fence for a few moments.

Calmly turn in the other direction and increase to the jog as you head back down the straight line to the opposite end of the arena. Because of the increased speed, your horse might dive left and right as he approaches the fence, wondering which way to go. It is important to quit

After initially walking your horse, pick a focal point on the fence and calmly trot straight to it while keeping his body in good frame.

As you near the fence, simply quit riding and let your horse stop and stand quietly for a few minutes.

riding your horse, as before, and try to keep him straight, quiet, and moving forward until he rests with his nose in close proximity to the fence. Getting after your horse for darting from side to side only increases his anxiety about fencing and worsens the problem. Calm, assertive guidance is the best way to help your horse understand the fencing concept, and he can come to like fencing when he knows a rest awaits him at the fence. After a few slow fencing repetitions, your horse can accept what is being asked of him and approach the fence with confidence and consistency.

"A good trainer is never in a hurry to show how fast his horse can run down the arena or how far his horse can slide...."

At this time, you can proceed to fence your horse at the lope, but as before, with the initial increase in speed, you might find your horse again diving left to right as he approaches the far wall. Calmly continue to show him the fence, just as you did at the jog, reaffirming the exercise and rebuilding your horse's confidence.

Once settled into working on a straight line, your horse, as most do, might start to slow as he runs out of arena near the fence. You can add a little drive to keep your horse loping through the last possible stride. That drive encourages the desired sit-down stop and causes your horse to round his body and tuck his nose to avoid colliding with the wall. Do not add so much forward impulsion that you spook your horse about fencing, only enough impulsion that he drives into his rundown and then sits down in the stop. The reward of rest goes a long way toward convincing your horse to comply. When your horse sits deeply into the stop at the wall, give him plentiful time to catch his breath and associate that break with his effort.

During the rundown, your horse should give readily to the hackamore and travel on a clean line without leaning his body or going off-lead. His speed should be consistent from

departure all the way to the fence, without him hurrying or slowing his pace at will.

After fencing your horse, if you find that he gets a little antsy when asked to lope, bring him to a walk. Work the hackamore in a bumping motion on his nose and continue to walk the length of the arena. You might have to walk back and forth several times to keep your horse from anticipating the lope departure and rundown. Ensure that you diffuse the situation each and every time your horse gets a little strong.

Allowing your hackamore horse to get even the slightest bit ahead of you one time is all it takes to teach him to run through his headgear. If you don't think you are sending your horse to the end of the arena, and it seems more like your horse is taking you there, you must bring him down to a walk immediately and regain control. Be very conscious not to pull steadily on the hackamore when your horse gets strong; instead, use the proper bumping action that works the hackamore on his nose and jaw. Even double him around to the side if necessary.

A good trainer is never in a hurry to show how fast his horse can run down the arena or how far his horse can slide; a horseman knows those things are the end results of a very disciplined program. A horseman focuses on his horse's correct carriage and the mechanics of each part in the sequence, knowing that if he loses the first step in the lope departure, he's lost everything.

When you ride with that same mentality and patience, fencing can help nurture and develop your horse's stopping ability and style, preparing him for a truly balanced, sliding stop away from the arena wall. As with the spin, every horse's charisma in the sliding stop varies. Just as the colored strands woven into a hackamore nose button create a design unlike any other, each horse comes into his own way of stopping. His design, or way of doing that, is not exactly like any other, but absolutely is the product of an artist's hands.

Developing the Slide

It is often said that a good horse approaching a stop runs "like he's going somewhere." If you understand what is meant by those words, you know they truly are a marvelous description of a willing stopper heading down to bury his hocks in the sand.

A horse that has been rushed, worried, or improperly trained to run down the pen often appears wide-eyed and tense, even going off-lead or charging through the hackamore or bridle. He runs as if he's going to come apart any second, and it's unclear where he might end up going. A horse like that is trying to outthink or second-guess what his rider is asking, ever anticipating the drive to the fence or the stop.

But a horse that has been shown proper stopping form through consistent, confidence-building training displays an entirely different demeanor. He gallops down the straight line, listens and waits for commands; always calm and relaxed, he is prepared to do as he's told. This horse travels as though he's unconfined by the arena's four walls. He lopes forward, seemingly unaware of the place his rider usually asks him to stop, and appears unfettered as he takes the last few strides into the fence. The horse gallops honestly, without cheat or fractiousness in him, as if he'd carry on unquestioningly in that wonderful frame all the way to the next town.

If you've spent your time wisely, your horse should run straight lines in this manner—freely and matter-of-factly. He should sit down over his hocks, even slide into the fence, willingly guided from his first

As desired, this horse moves freely, yet relaxed in the rundown without appearing to be rushed and without anticipating the coming stop.

At this point the horse has mastered the fundamentals and is ready to stop away from the wall, but he's not yet ready to approach the stop with blazing speed.

step to the last. He has been fenced at varying speeds, and he can perform with the same soft carriage at a fast pace that he does at a slow one.

Now your horse is ready to be stopped near the end of the rundown and away from the wall. However, when your horse increases his speed, if he elevates his nose and pushes it out of the desirable frame, it's time to regress in order to regain your lost control of the basics used in stopping. To continue training on your horse's stop when some of the fundamentals are beginning to unravel is of huge consequence, and one that eventually can destroy the very core of your hackamore horse. Trouble-shooting throughout your course of training is a must and requires that

you be vigilant about the details. As is true of any good horseman, you always must be willing to take a few steps backward in the name of progress.

Stop in the Open

When you are ready to stop your horse away from the wall, set out as you would when fencing. Choose a medium speed at which your horse is most confident. Consider your horse's way of going as you gallop down the line. Is he soft in the hackamore? Is he running a true, straight line, respectfully maintaining his speed?

Often when a rider sets his mind to stop, he becomes so fixated on the upcoming slide that he forsakes the golden rules of the rundown. By doing so, he not only sets himself up for immediate failure, but also for long-term failure. In a matter of only a couple of repetitions, a horse can learn to barrel down the arena to a stop, out of form, which eventually leads to a run-off.

You can decide to stop your galloping horse at any time, but be savvy enough to decide not to stop him if things don't go well along the way. The stop is a product of the rundown, so do not bother to say whoa at the end of a substandard rundown unless a poor quality stop is what you're after.

Here's how your rundown and stop in the open should go.

A substantial reward of rest and slack reins should be awarded your horse for his effort.

If this is the first slide he's performed away from the wall on the straightaway, end the session there for the day. He then remembers that his compliance is worthwhile.

It's a transgression to gallop your horse back and forth, stopping again and again, this early in development. Your horse can be soured to the stop, just as he can come to resent the spin, and a host of problems arise from overdoing the stop. Scotching, or anticipating, is one such negative that can be taught to a horse by poor riding habits. A young horse also can become frazzled, afraid, or resentful of his work, not to mention sore, when stopping is overdone.

A common occurrence, one for which many riders spend a lot of time punishing

As your horse nears the three-quarter point of his rundown, he should gallop freely and travel straight toward the fence, without anticipation or worry.

As you sit, say whoa and soften your body, and take your feet slightly away from your horse's sides. Your horse, properly conditioned to the stop command, then can balance over his hocks and fold into the ground without taking his nose away from the hackamore.

their horses, happens when a horse roots out his nose as he comes to a stop. Unfortunately for the horse, this rooting condition is man-made, but an oblivious rider hasn't enough wherewithal to assess the problem.

Very often, a split-second before a rider sits and gives the whoa command, his hands close around the rein, taking away a fraction of slack. No matter how miniscule an amount that might seem, the horse feels the change and eventually pushes out his nose and lays into the rider's closed hands. Any rider must maintain that necessary life in his fingers in all aspects of riding, including the stop. A dead, or inactive, hand on the hackamore is equivalent to a pull on the hackamore, and a pull on the hackamore is returned by a pull from the horse.

In the event of a weak-hearted or problematic stop, ensure that you are not giving your horse something to pull against. Take hold of one rein of the hackamore, then bump the other alternately—a good method of working the mecate rein. Back your horse off the hackamore or even roll him over his hocks, if necessary, to remind him of the face-to-foot connection he must respect at all times.

Have patience as you work through stopping problems. Dissect the issues you face by again working through the foundation exercises that have gotten you to the point where you are now. By reminding your horse of the core fundamentals and of the hackamore's authority, your chance of ending your session on a good note improves greatly. By taking control and reestablishing that face-to-foot connection, you win the fight even though you might not have gotten the stop you desired on the straightaway. Chances are, due to this approach, your horse comes back with an improved response the next riding session.

You can no more force your horse's learning than you can alter the hands of time. When working on an intricate design, a rawhide artisan takes breaks periodically to relieve frustration, so that he can be at his very best when working. Doing so is of even greater importance to you as a horse trainer for you deal not with inanimate strings, but with an animal that has feelings, physical limitations, and free will.

Whenever you have a problem performing these exercises, go back and revisit the basics until your horse regains his composure before moving on to work on a new skill.

"Giving a horse a job of any kind helps him to relate his rider's commands to reasons for compliance."

8

Overcoming Challenges

Throughout training, regardless of the level of talent a horse possesses, many setbacks and stumbling blocks emerge. These challenges are a natural part of the learning process by which horsemen sculpt broke horses into being. Some animals, just as with humans, have more passive personalities than others and are easy to train. The resistance they offer is generally simple and short-lived in comparison to that of fiery, spirited horses.

Although some trainers in today's industry have the luxury of culling the temperamental colts from their programs, in general, most trainers must make a living with prospects that are less than the cream of the crop. However, fine champions have been forged from beginnings laden with resistance, and these horses owe their success to the trainers willing to step up to the challenge. If a horse has a good mentality and athleticism, a creative trainer can outsmart resistance as it arises, eventually harnessing the horse's body and mind into a workable form.

When meeting challenges with your horse, first analyze yourself in the face of difficulty. Then you can rule out any problems that might be directly related to improper balance or incorrect cueing on your part.

Run through a checklist in your mind, covering everything from your balance in the saddle to your hands on the mecate. If all these points check out okay, and you're confident that you're doing your part correctly, it's time to backtrack a bit and examine your training course from past to present. Make sure that nothing has been rushed or skipped along the way, as that could be the source of the setbacks you now face.

Often going back to the basics of proper cueing and using good hands alleviates the rider's concerns when meeting resistance. In revisiting the steps previously taken to establish the all-important core principle of that face-to-foot connection, a horse can be worked through many forms of resistance without additional measures needing to be taken. In other cases, however, some horses decide to cheat or to fight without any error on the rider's part. A few of the following tips and tricks can provide help for a good hand dealing with a difficult horse.

The Lead Rope as a Training Aid

In the bitting-up exercises performed on the longe line early in the training program, the lead rope of the mecate rein has been used to create a barrier for

Longeing another horse not only gives your riding horse a job, but also allows him to focus on another animal when cattle aren't available.

a horse to bump if he pops his nose out of position. This same aid can be utilized when riding a horse that likes to root his nose into the hackamore as he stops or performs other maneuvers.

Note that this technique should not be used if you find yourself running short on patience. A bad-tempered teacher can't school a horse well. Remaining calm and cool gets you through the challenge faster and better than engaging in a war with an opponent who outweighs you six to one.

How to use the mecate lead as a training aid when you're horseback is shown below.

Run the lead of the mecate between your horse's front legs and up the left side of your saddle.

When you're mounted, hold the lead rope as you ride. You can work the lead in conjunction with your left hand on the mecate, creating an effect that encourages your horse to keep his nose on the vertical.

When asking your horse to stop, leave the lead rope set in your hand without pulling on the lead. As with the previous bitting-up exercise, when your horse roots his nose out of position, he hits the lead, as if it's a tie-down. The lead corrects him for rooting out his nose and overstepping the boundary.

After a couple of such repetitions, your horse respects the barrier and keeps his nose tucked when loping and stopping to avoid contact with the hackamore. You also can check the lead rope as you back your horse to further encourage the desired softness.

Give Your Horse Purpose

Going back to industry roots reminds everyone that horses of yesteryear were working animals. From day one under saddle, they were given tasks, and all training they encountered came by way of their jobs. Horses today don't often experience training that translates directly into obvious necessity. Without ground to cover, cattle to move, and natural obstacles to navigate, riders today are left in enclosures, going around and around, trying to convince their horses to do what often must seem pointless to the horses.

Many forms of resistance are due directly to this problem—the horse sees no purpose in what he does and feels the human on his back demands that the horse expend energy for nothing. Giving a horse a job of any kind helps him to relate his rider's commands to reasons for compliance. Very often a rider can take the argument out of a horse by giving him purpose, no matter how simple the purpose might be.

Working cows offers a horse reasons to turn left and right, to stop and back, using his body in balance from his nose to his hocks. When he stops poorly or turns heavily, he falls out of proper position on the cow and directly relates the schooling the rider gives to this error. If the horse has any desire and aptitude, he tries hard the next time, using himself in better form. Rather than feeling as if he has been bullied or spurred for nothing, the horse instead thinks about the job and relates to why it's important to perform correctly. Though his rider asks for the same body carriage with the same cues used in dry work, the horse's changed mentality when he works cattle makes all the difference. Less resentment equals greater improvement.

Giving your horse a real job, in other words, a reason to perform a maneuver, helps keep him mentally fresh, more willing to perform and less resentful of his training.

Horseback Longeing

If you do not have access to cows, there are other good jobs to give your horse to help further his training process. Longeing a horse while riding your horse is a great exercise. Doing this gives your horse another animal for focus and also demands that your horse remain aware of the longe line as he moves about the pen.

In order to succeed with this exercise, it goes without saying that your mount must work fairly well under saddle and that secondary horse should be decent on the longe line. This longeing task requires a little coordination to perfect, but shapes up relatively quickly with practice.

As you send the longe horse counterclockwise to the left around you, guide your hackamore horse in a circle to the left so that the longe line stays on his right side. If your horse lags a bit, the longe horse's movement draws the line against your horse's neck and jowl, encouraging his responsiveness to your mecate rein aid on the circle. You are offered the opportunity to both rein and rate your mount as you longe, and he is given an object, the longe horse, to associate with your demands.

When longeing another horse to the left, your horse should guide softly off the rein, focusing on the other animal and the line. Your right leg helps maneuver your horse in proper form around the circle. Hold the line low enough that, should the longe horse bolt, the line presses against your mount's neck, forcing him to move into position. In a matter of time, your horse learns to read the longe line and to move accordingly on his own, a concept directly related to neck-reining.

Both animals should move quietly and comfortably for several circles before you ask them to stop. This procedure, being new to both horses, can be a little clumsy in the beginning, but with time flows more smoothly. Have patience as you work both animals in relation to each other, and focus on teaching your hackamore horse to move swiftly and softly off your cues.

When you reverse the horses, coil the line as you ride to the other side of the longe horse and reposition yourself to send that longe horse away in the opposite direction. It might take some doing to get the longe horse to stand still while riding your mount around the other horse. Make sure you take whatever time is needed. If you experience a good, concrete session the first time, insisting that the longe horse perform with the same manners he has when you're afoot, tomorrow's session can go much better.

When you're ready to send the longe horse around you again, this time in the other direction, rein your mount around to follow and lift the line over his head to work the longe horse off the other side of your horse's body. This is a great opportunity to sneak in a rollback, or you can even back a few steps and

After making several circles, stop the horses. Once both horses are completely stopped, ride to the opposite side of the longe horse, coiling the line neatly as you go. It might be necessary to make small checks on the line to keep the longe horse standing still until you're in position to send him away in the other direction.

Position yourself in front of the longe horse, allowing ample space between the horses, or to the longe horse's right if he's facing you. Then cluck once to move him onto a right-hand circle. You can then do a rollback or back and turn your mount to the right to follow. Raise your hand to bring the line over your mount's head as you rein him around the turn, carefully watching the longe horse as you proceed. Keep a safe distance between the horses and do not allow slack in the longe line. If it settles to the ground, it could tangle around either animal's legs.

then turn, depending on the ability level of your mount.

Once these basics are going well, you can open up from your circle to send the longe horse in a straight line around a large enclosure, such as an arena, by riding after the other horse a bit. As you do, your hackamore horse listens to your cues and relates them to the animal he's controlling. Your horse allows you to rate his speed, to stop him, and to turn him while he focuses on the job. It's almost as if you sneak the training into your horse, without him even realizing what you're doing. Aside from that benefit, this exercise is also a great break from the ordinary for both your riding horse and the horse on the longe line.

See the Opportunities

If you open your eyes to the training opportunities that exist all around, you can find creative ways to teach your horse in a very constructive manner. Something as simple as opening a gate gives purpose to your leg and rein cues, which your horse readily can understand. The basic mechanics of the situation are of benefit. The gate coming toward him teaches your horse to side-pass with less demanding cues from your leg and spur than would be necessary when asking him to side-pass in the middle of the arena.

> # "...while he focuses on the job. It's almost as if you sneak the training into your horse...."

When you want to longe a horse on the straightaway, control the longe horse by moving up to position your mount just behind the longe horse's shoulder and off to one side, rather than riding directly behind the other horse. Monitor both horses, and when necessary, check the longe line to communicate the desired rate of speed as you continue longeing. Properly executed, longeing another horse builds your horse's confidence in your commands by giving purpose to half-turns and to rating his speed, as well as to his stops and backing.

Be thoughtful in your training approach at all times and ever creative in resolving challenges. Seek to convince your horse that fulfilling your command is beneficial to him as a partner, not as a fearful servant.

Less very often is more when training. Demanding too much too soon ruins many good horses every year, and the lack of human compassion and empathy is far too common. Imagine being in a gym, coached by a trainer speaking in a foreign language. For days, the coach gives orders you struggle to understand, and only by his reactions to your attempts to perform are you able to start figuring out what he wants. Just as your mind begins to clue into his reactions, your body grows exhausted from the drills, making it even more difficult for you to perform as the coach expects. You try to explain that you're weary and sore, but the language barrier leaves your complaints to fall on deaf ears. The only hope you have is this foreigner's compassion and understanding of your circumstance—either that or you could fight.

That situation is similar to the frustrating interaction many horses experience with their riders. By nature, the horse is a helper, known throughout history as a beast of burden for his service to man. He flourishes when given a job to do, and does that job without failing or fighting when he's rewarded fairly for his effort.

Knowing when enough is enough is as important to training your horse as knowing what to do and when to do it. All the best training sessions in the world are nothing without rest. If you get tough on a horse for being clumsy in the turnaround or weak in his stop, and the horse is physically sore, his performance only gets worse, and he learns to hate being ridden. Make sure your horse has ample time to heal his body and rebuild worked muscles. Then you reduce the risk of mistakenly thinking that your horse is saying, "I won't," when he really means, "I can't."

"... you always must remember to aspire to greatness, yet be satisfied with your horse's individual best."

9

Working Cattle

It is spellbinding to watch a good horse, with little visible aid from his rider, work on a soft rein and control a cow. The unmatched intensity in the horse's expression and the coil and spring of every muscle is awe-inspiring. A great cow horse displays the athleticism of an acrobat, the finesse of a ballerina, and the power of a National Football League linebacker. A cow horse is the ultimate athlete.

With deep respect, a trained eye admires the level of training that has gone into such a horse. The horse's huge, physical moves represent hours upon hours of precise schooling that have set his form, as if it is cemented in the horse's mind. Every muscle responsible for every move the horse makes so effortlessly has been conditioned from day one under saddle. This horse is the product of a true artisan, one who understands all the elements of preparation, procedure, and well-spent time.

The great cow horse is born, needing only to be shaped and refined by a savvy trainer, and not many horses fall into this esteemed category. However, an average horse can be made into a good one when a rider applies solid training principles.

The exercises and drills you've used to build your hackamore horse into a light, willing partner already have set the stage for his development as

a cow horse. The core of his hackamore training has conditioned him to use his hocks with strength, round his spine and yield his nose. His progression as a working horse now depends on the level of his inborn drive, your ability to read cattle, and your keen awareness, which never lets your horse sacrifice proper form.

Introducing Cattle

When your horse is first introduced to cow work, a quiet, soft cow should be used. One that's too fresh and wild is far more than a green horse can handle and can shake his confidence. A cow that's been overworked and soured does not make a good candidate either. You want to choose an animal that is respectful, yet has some life, while being slow enough that your green horse can trot or lope slowly as he works.

Every horse, regardless of breeding, has his own level of inborn "cow." Generally a horse that has a little fear or respect for the cow watches intently, working with bright eyes and ears in the desired fashion. Although some horses naturally are very expressive and reactionary, the average horse depends greatly on a good rider to help tune him into the cow's subtle movements.

All your previous work has developed and conditioned your horse physically and mentally to be a willing partner in cattle work.

As you approach the cow at a walk, pay attention to the small details that lend clues as to what the cow is about to do. If the cow flicks an ear, stop your horse and break-off in a quarter-turn immediately. The cow might respond to your horse's movement by making a turn away from your horse or even do something as subtle as dropping its

As you step toward the cow, your green horse should be alert and show interest in the cow as this young horse does.

As the cow lowers its head in preparation to make a move, promptly stop your mount to help set your horse up for the coming action.

head. In either case, break your horse back through a half-turn to teach him to react to whatever motion the cow offers. With repetition, your green horse clues into and seeks those subtle changes in the cow's face and body, and that's what gives your horse that bright-eyed, pricked-ear, bird-dog-on-a-point expression.

Then break your horse off in a quarter-turn to the right, as shown here. He already has the solid foundation to balance on his hocks and sweep his front end around lightly. When the cow makes another move away from your horse, you again initiate whatever action necessary.

Obviously a few well-executed turns have drawn this expressive, alert young horse to the cow; however, overly agressive behavior in a horse should be curtailed promptly.

Tracking cattle slowly gives a horse time to learn how to hold a position on a cow.

Push and Rate

The three components of successful cow-horse work are push, rate, and turn. Once you've introduced your horse to cattle and he shows an aptitude for the sport, he can be taught the first two of these three elements.

Tracking a cow, or driving it, teaches your green horse to hook up with the cow, watch its movements and be guided about the pen while pushing, or driving, the other animal. When doing this work and learning to track a cow, your horse also becomes aware of rating his speed as the cow slows or accelerates. If your horse has any desire at all, he should hook up to the cow pretty readily. Soft slack in the mecate rewards the horse when he's in position on the cow and doing his job.

Circling

After you've tracked a cow a few laps and if you're working a good cow, one that's not too fast or wild for a green horse, you should be able to ride up to the animal's shoulder to circle the cow. Circling gives your young horse confidence in his control of the cow and builds your horse's desire to turn the cow.

Good form is key here, and your horse never should be allowed to drop his shoulder and lean into the turn as he circles. When a horse drops his shoulder, he offsets or counterbalances that by swinging his hip away from the circle. This causes him to cross-lead as he lopes, and he loses the necessary rear-end-drive.

Instead, your horse should remain in proper form with an aligned body, which allows him to drive from his hocks while keeping his front end light. Another factor of great importance: Your horse never should be reined into a cow in a manner that pulls your horse's nose out of position and away from the cow. Doing so destroys the appropriate body alignment and begins a bad habit, not to mention that doing so also pulls your horse's focus off the cow.

When a horse in perfect position calmly tracks a cow around the arena, it's time for the next step and circling a cow. Notice the rider's hands on the mecate are soft and allow the colt to try to be cowy; soft hands help or correct a horse only when necessary.

When the cow slows, the rider moves his horse into position to circle by riding up to the cow's shoulder. The reins offer slack when the horse finds the correct position, and with repetition this reward teaches the horse to hunt the circle. When the maneuver is accurately performed, as the horse circles the cow, the horse's body cups lightly around the cow—reading, rating and pushing the cow as necessary.

Turning on the Fence

If you take your time and train with patience, your horse's confidence can grow. His desire to work and his instincts about cattle build with each good session. By never placing unrealistic demands on a green horse, you find progress in steady increments with fewer setbacks. Just as the sliding stop is the result of many exercises developed with time, the big fencing turns of the working cow horse are the result of slow, smart craftsmanship.

Remember: Only after the first two components of the cow horse, push and rate, are in play is your horse ready to go past the cow and turn it on the fence.

To introduce your horse to turning on the fence, ride your horse into position to drive the cow down the wall, staying close to the animal's side. When you feel your horse reads and rates the cow as he should, ask your horse to go by the cow and keep your horse's nose toward the cow as he passes. Since your horse already has been circling cattle, he drives up to the cow, is willing to cup around and control the cow, which can help pull the horse through a turn on the fence.

After the turn, if your horse ends up between the wall and the cow, you can head to the center of the arena and circle the cow and encourage your horse's drive to contain the other animal. If the cow comes out of the turn and stays on the fence, again ride up to the driving position and take the cow down your fence for a few strides before you go by the cow a second time. Give your horse rest

Training a horse to turn a cow on the fence is similar to achieving any high-level maneuver—slow, steady, confidence-building sessions lead to success.

when he does his job well. Pitch some slack in the mecate and allow him to breathe. A good pat on the rump or neck goes a long way, too.

Common Problems

At any point in time that your hackamore horse tries to adhere to a cow and really stick with the cow against your wishes, you should strongly back your horse off the cow. Your horse must understand that, no matter how great his desire is to work, your authority as his rider governs.

Once your horse has grasped the idea of tracking a cow, pull your horse off the track by sitting down in your saddle and taking hold of one rein and bumping the other—in that order. Do not take hold of the hackamore without first giving the quit command by sitting down in your saddle, and just as important, do not pull solidly with both hands on the mecate, or your horse might run through the hackamore. If necessary, back your horse to soften his poll and even turn him around a few revolutions. At all costs, regardless of speed or his drive to work, he must respect your commands.

It also is important that you do not wait for your horse to become headstrong before pulling him off cattle for the first time. Choose a time when your horse is performing well, in good driving position, and sit him down on his hocks. At some point in cow work, you need this emergency brake, and a rider who has trained it into his horse properly has a far better outcome than the one who has not.

Occasionally some horses try to bite cattle when they come into contact. This behavior is unacceptable and should be curtailed promptly. The hackamore itself discourages an overly aggressive, mouthy colt from biting in much the same way a cavesson or noseband does.

You even can add an extra wrap on the mecate above the heel knot if you are riding a hackamore fairly loose on your horse's muzzle. A more snug fit inhibits the horse, which helps prevent him from committing the infraction. The hackamore is a great help with this problem, not only because the hackamore directly relates to the offending part of the horse's body, but also because the horse doesn't have to be pulled off the cow to be reprimanded by his rider. The sting of the hackamore's nose button and shanks directly relate to the horse opening his mouth, and he thinks twice about trying that again.

Focus on the Goal

Often when thinking about the legendary working horses, everyone naturally hopes the colt he rides might resemble such a horse if only in a small way. The great hackamore horses, such as Johnny Tivio, give everyone something to which to aspire. In all fairness, however, keep in mind that the supernatural talent of the industry giants is born only in a few horses. Nonetheless, the average cow horse can be made into a good, solid, reliable mount that folks admire in a different way. He need not be "wowing" a crowd to be valuable.

> **"A hackamore horse, just like a hackamore, doesn't have to be the fanciest to be prized..."**

Although everyone looks back fondly, even with awe, at such cow horses as Mitch—the way he could run wide-open down the fence and absolutely devour a cow in a turn—you always must remember to aspire to greatness, yet be satisfied with your horse's individual best. Solid blue-collar horses, whose work ethic and consistency shine, have made many wins. Time and again such horses have proven to be capable partners because of their matter-of-fact approach to their work and their reliability.

No matter the level of a horse's talent, the training approach you take can work to make a willing, responsive partner of the next equine superstar, as well as a less talented, but hardworking horse. Either way, reward your horse for his small improvements, and you find he comes into form with a happy, willing spirit. A hackamore horse, just like a hackamore, doesn't have to be the fanciest to be prized; he simply has to be developed with proper techniques and perform consistently with honest, workmanlike appeal.

"The most sensitive part of the horse is the bars of his mouth. When he's young, the bars are soft, and once you bruise them, they callus; lose feeling. The best way to sum it up—the hackamore saves the horse's mouth for the bridle."
—Bobby Ingersol

10

Vaquero Methods: Snaffle, Hackamore, Bridle and Variations

In the land of mañana, vaqueros didn't have books to reference about training horses. No one held clinics on Sundays or lessons on weekday afternoons. The horse-training means and methods the vaqueros used came to them through firsthand experience and often in the school of hard knocks. Though they had customary ways of breaking colts, the vaqueros understood the necessity of creative problem-solving. Working with the tough, range-raised horse of that time led the vaqueros to try different ways of taming wild-spirited 5-year-old horses.

For example, sometimes a horse, after being snubbed to the post for saddling, was towed out and away from the corrals into the open. Such a potentially violent bronc was led by a rope around the front foot, as that the easiest way to control the horse. Once the horse was away from the corrals, a large, heavy log was tied by a long rope to the hackamore. The wild, dangerous horse was then left for a day to sort out things himself. He came to respect the hackamore after a few temper fits, trying to jerk free or drag the log, and by the time a vaquero came to retrieve the horse, he was quite willing.

Modern horses, handled from younger ages and softer in constitution, do not require such methods to mold them into willing partners. Although the traditionalist might argue that a pure hackamore man always starts his colts in the hackamore, there is

Hackamore horsemanship reflects only a portion of the time-honored traditions used to develop a true bridle horse.

certainly room for creative problem-solving in every training program. Not all colts come to be good, broke horses by exactly the same string of events. Likewise, every trainer has different talents and limitations with different horses and various pieces of equipment.

Using methods that work for you and your horse as individuals is first and foremost in importance. If you have been starting colts in the snaffle and are new to the hackamore, a variation to the hackamore introduction method previously described might be a comfortable fit for you.

Quatro Riendas

The *quatro riendas,* or four-rein, is a combination training method for introducing the hackamore to a snaffle-started colt without quitting the snaffle cold turkey. Just as the name implies, the four-rein setup involves working two separate sets of reins, which are controlled by both of the rider's hands.

This system begins by allowing the horse to carry the hackamore while being ridden in the snaffle, with the rider gradually beginning to use the mecate along with the snaffle reins. Ultimately, the colt is weaned from the bit and ridden exclusively in the hackamore.

As with any training process, the quatro-riendas approach requires time, patience, and consistency. This is not a shortcut to putting the horse in the hackamore by any means, just a different route to the same destination. The four-rein method not only demands skilled, nimble hands, but also a very attentive, intuitive trainer.

If you train forcefully, or with heavy, dull pulls on the hackamore simply because the snaffle is there to bail you out of a wreck, you're in for a rude awakening. If you teach your horse to disrespect, pull against, or fear the hackamore, when you then take off the snaffle bit, you might as well be driving a car with no steering wheel or brakes.

The same good training principles outlined in earlier pages must be in play for the quatro-riendas method to work. Good hands on the mecate, working in the bump-and-release application, also must give a signal, the command, a consequence, and then a reward.

In the quatro-riendas setup, the hackamore is placed on the horse first, with the snaffle put over the hackamore, on top of it. This ensures the correct fit that allows both the bit and the hackamore to work properly without interfering with one another. A common mistake in this configuration is setting the hackamore too low on the horse's nose. Not only does this hinder function of the headgear, but the snaffle bit also can pinch the corners of a horse's mouth against the shanks of the hackamore.

Riding with the Four-Rein

With the quatro riendas, all the same training principles and exercises outlined previously again should be introduced to your horse while you gradually work less from the snaffle bit and more from the hackamore until your horse works solely off the hackamore. This transition takes place during the course of many rides, not just one or two. Even after your horse is going well in the hackamore, you might leave the snaffle in place with the reins looped over the horn as an insurance policy for a few additional rides.

To make the transition from the snaffle to the hackamore, initially perform a tight, walking circle, for example, with the snaffle bit giving the main cue, and the mecate creating minimal movement to the hackamore.

In time, gradually equalize the lengths of the reins and the mecate, so the cues come to your horse by the hackamore and the snaffle together. Since your horse feels the snaffle, to which he's accustomed, along with the new sensation of the hackamore, he's relatively comfortable following his nose.

With time and patience, you then gradually wean your horse off the snaffle until the bridle reins are slack. Then, while you use only the hackamore, your horse can perform a perfectly framed 15-foot walking circle.

Los Dos Riendas

The transitional phase between riding a horse in the hackamore and straight-up in the bridle is called *las dos riendas,* or the two-rein, the final process of refinement a horse must go through in the traditional training method. The two-rein bridges the gap between the hackamore and bridle and, when utilized properly, unites the two in a seamless progression. As when a rawhide braider ties the shanks of the hackamore into the heel knot, the two-rein is the finishing touch that ties all the preliminary training into a state of completion.

If you've been a diligent student of the art of hackamore training, when the time of las dos riendas comes around, your horse should

The mecate must be set to a length that enables you to hold it in conjunction with the bridle reins and without any sloppy excess. You can close your fist around both reins together, or not, as you prefer.

Initially, some trainers prefer to ride the two-rein with fingers between the reins, working up to the closed grip as a horse advances in his training.

be more than ready for the change. Two years in the hackamore have taught him all the skills required in a finished horse, including neck-reining with true collection and balanced carriage.

A light ⅜-inch *bosalito* now replaces his hackamore with the curb bridle fitted on top. The traditional spade bit provides a roller or cricket against which your horse can slide his tongue back and forth. This encourages the natural chewing and licking behavior that a horse demonstrates when relaxing his jaw and settling into a task.

Riding and training in the two-rein is a gradual progression to working your horse solely off the bridle. When you first begin the change, allow your horse to carry the bit, even without the reins attached, as you work from the bosalito. Give your horse time to

learn to hold the spade bit and to mouth the cricket, as this makes him more receptive to commands once you pick up the bridle reins.

When the two sets of reins are first in play, it is important to set the mecate shorter than the romal reins to ensure that the majority of your cues come from the bosalito. Allow your horse to feel the bit lightly in the early phases of the two-rein, then gradually increase the bridle contact until both the mecate and reins are equally engaged. This process is accomplished with time and many riding sessions, with only a little additional bridle contact initiated daily.

Riding With the Two-Rein

When riding your horse in the two-rein, keep in mind that this is a transitional phase, so keep things simple. At times you might

Introduce your horse to the two-rein by asking him to perform familiar, comfortable routines and giving him time to become equally comfortable with the bit in his mouth.

find it necessary to reach down with your right or left hand to work the reins, or even the mecate by itself. Keep your horse loose, soft, and responsive by never overusing the bridle or hauling hard on your horse's mouth.

Work the old familiar drills that built the solid foundation of your hackamore horse and revisit these exercises as you introduce the bridle in the two-rein setup. By starting with the simple walking and jogging circles, you allow your horse a comfort zone in which he can think through the new sensations he feels.

Initially, for example, guide your green two-rein horse in a small circle, allowing him to feel soft bridle contact as he gives to the bosalito.

After several circles, make a little more contact to engage the bridle reins, which allows your horse to feel the bridle distinctly. The mecate and the reins are almost equal here, with the mecate giving only a slightly stronger cue. Always utilize good hands on both sets of reins.

You now must give your horse time to think through what he's experiencing, but soon your horse relaxes into the circle and performs with proper form.

Once your horse is comfortable in the two-rein, working quietly in good form at the walk, jog, and lope, you can begin the circle-and-turn exercises. If your horse stiffens during any portion of the drills, go immediately to the hackamore to soften your horse's response.

Though the two-rein is a new phase of training, all of the same solid basics apply, and these are the very components that get you out of a wreck should things fall apart with your horse.

The same calm, cool handling of the mecate must be ever-present in your transition to the bridle. Lose your patience

When you use the two-rein to ask your horse to perform a spin, your green horse might begin turning in fairly good form. However, feeling the bridle engage in this exercise for the first time, your horse might stiffen slightly after the initial response, as does the horse in the photo.

You then take hold of the mecate, letting the bridle rein have just a little more slack, and bump your horse around the turn for a couple revolutions. Once your horse softly yields, relax all commands and let the horse come to a stop. When you again ask for a turnaround, your horse should respond to the two-rein with more of the desired softness, carriage and form than before.

even once, and you might pay for it ever after when your horse is in the bridle. It is of utmost importance that you remember your bridle, when engaged, must connect the horse's face to his hind feet, just as the hackamore does.

In every drill you perform, use the lightest cue possible before you resort to strong aids. Give your horse a chance to do things right before you start schooling him. If you've prepared your horse properly in the hackamore, a little help from the bosalito can initiate the correct softness in the bridle.

Choose the setting of your reins wisely, varying the hackamore-to-bridle ratio to be pertinent to each situation at hand. From one maneuver to the next, you might change from working your horse with the romal rein and revert back to working him solely with the mecate. The trainer who sees fine results in the two-rein is the one who understands that delicate balance, and is willing to dance back and forth between the two. Just as with the hackamore, you cannot muscle a horse into the bridle; you must show him how to be

there and why being straight-up in the bridle is a good place to be. Successfully making this transition from the hackamore requires patience and consistency.

As time passes, your horse in the two-rein setup comes to perform all the exercises, including cattle work, with less contact necessary on the hackamore. As in all stages of training, however, if you rush this final, transitional phase, your end result is not the sought-after bridle horse you desire. You must help your horse avoid bad habits in the bridle by taking your time and utilizing the sound principles you previously applied in the hackamore work. Good hands on the reins of a bit are just as important as they are on the mecate of a hackamore.

The true bridle horse, working in ideal form between the reins, is a testimony to years of persistence, patience, and applied wisdom. His grace, carriage, and athleticism demonstrate a freedom of movement that cannot be forced into being. The bridle horse is a work of art, cultivated by the hands of an artist through many miles and many seasons.

With time, your horse becomes seasoned to and comfortable with the two-rein—well on his way to becoming a true bridle horse.

In Closing

Upon reflection, we find great knowledge in the traditions of our reinsmen forefathers. Their ways of life, now barely more than memories, still echo in the footfalls of our modern working horses. A true hackamore man hears that faint sound like a call to action, reminding him that he holds a place in the long line of his vaquero heritage.

Thirst for that knowledge and love of its history should be as much a part of your hackamore training program as the riding exercises and drills. Though the times, horses, and dress codes certainly have changed, every time you work a horse, you become a link in the hackamore's legacy. By training with passion and a sense of mañana, you help ensure the survival of the art of hackamore training in today's fast-paced world.

There is no shortcut to making a true hackamore horse, only the compilation of training time well-spent. The drills outlined here lead to success only when carried out by a tactful technician—one who understands the physical, mental, and emotional boundaries of his equine counterpart. Perhaps the greatest secret of the hackamore man isn't a particular technique or exercise at all—just a little thing called patience.

As you seat the hackamore on your horse's nose, survey the braided strands with admiration and respect. Let the hackamore itself stand as a reminder of the artistic process of building a hackamore horse. Each time you take up the mecate, allow the feel of la jaquima into your heart. Lose your impatience to its principles, and reset your clock to the ticking of a simpler time. Many great influences, both human and equine, have left their marks on the hackamore. Their spirits remain as if braided into the rawhide with the rich colors of the past, as well as with whispers of wisdom for the future.

Author Profile

Deanna Lally

Deanna Lally's passion for horses was evident early on. Most of her childhood entertainment revolved around Breyer® models, equestrian magazines, and the persistent sketching of horses. Her love for horses only developed with time, and now, as a trainer of reining horses, Lally competes and coaches students in American Quarter Horse Association shows, as well as National Reining Horse Association competitions, throughout the Pacific Northwest. On the side, she is a western artist, who still favors the horse as her prime subject for gallery exhibition, illustration and portraiture.